Issues in
Biomedical
Ethics

Other books in the Contemporary Issues series:

Environment
Sports

Issues in
Biomedical
Ethics

by Lisa Yount

Lucent Books, San Diego, CA

To the young people
who will have to make
tomorrow's hard decisions

Library of Congress Cataloging-in-Publication Date

Yount, Lisa.
    Issues in biomedical ethics / by Lisa Yount
      p. cm.—(Contemporary issues)
    Includes bibliographic references and index.
    Summary: Examines some of the ethical questions raised by the capabilities of modern science, in such areas as health care allocation, the hastening of a patient's death, the use of animals in research, and the altering of human genes.
    ISBN 1-56006-476-5 (alk. paper)
    1. Medical ethics—Juvenile literature. 2. Bioethics—Juvenile literature. [1. Medical ethics. 2. Bioethics.] I. Title. II. Series: Contemporary issues (San Diego, Calif.)
R724.Y73 1998
174'.2—dc21   97-30784
                                      CIP
                                      AC

TABLE OF CONTENTS

Foreword

When men are brought face to face with their opponents, forced to listen and learn and mend their ideas, they cease to be children and savages and begin to live like civilized men. Then only is freedom a reality, when men may voice their opinions because they must examine their opinions.

Walter Lippmann, American editor and writer

CONTROVERSY FOSTERS DEBATE. The very mention of a controversial issue prompts listeners to choose sides and offer opinion. But seeing beyond one's opinions is often difficult. As Walter Lippmann implies, true reasoning comes from the ability to appreciate and understand a multiplicity of viewpoints. This ability to assess the range of opinions is not innate; it is learned by the careful study of an issue. Those who wish to reason well, as Lippmann attests, must be willing to examine their own opinions even as they weigh the positive and negative qualities of the opinions of others.

The *Contemporary Issues* series explores controversial topics through the lens of opinion. The series addresses some of today's most debated issues and, drawing on the diversity of opinions, presents a narrative that reflects the controversy surrounding those issues. All of the quoted testimonies are taken from primary sources and represent both prominent and lesser-known persons who have argued these topics. For example, the title on biomedical ethics contains the views of physicians commenting on both sides of the physician-assisted suicide issue: Some wage a moral argument that assisted suicide allows patients to die with dignity, while others assert that assisted suicide violates the Hippocratic oath. Yet the book also includes the opinions of those who see the issue in a more personal way. The relative of a person who died by assisted suicide feels the loss of a loved one and makes a plaintive cry against it, while companions of another assisted suicide victim attest that their friend no longer wanted to endure the agony of a slow death. The profusion of quotes illustrates the range of thoughts and emotions that impinge on any debate. Displaying the range of perspectives, the series is designed to show how personal belief—whether informed by statistical evidence, religious conviction, or public opinion—shapes and complicates arguments.

Each title in the *Contemporary Issues* series discusses multiple controversies within a single field of debate. The title on environmental issues, for example, contains one chapter that asks whether the Endangered Species Act should be repealed, while another asks if Americans can afford the economic and social costs of environmentalism. Narrowing the focus of debate to a specific question, each chapter sharpens the competing perspectives and investigates the philosophies and personal convictions that inform these viewpoints.

Students researching contemporary issues will find this format particularly useful in uncovering the central controversies of topics by placing them in a moral, economic, or political context that allows the students to easily see the points of disagreement. Because of this structure, the series provides an excellent launching point for further research. By clearly defining major points of contention, the series also aids readers in critically examining the structure and source of debates. While providing a resource on which to model persuasive essays, the quoted opinions also permit students to investigate the credibility and usefulness of the evidence presented.

For students contending with current issues, the ability to assess the credibility, usefulness, and persuasiveness of the testimony as well as the factual evidence given by the quoted experts is critical not only in judging the merits of these arguments but in analyzing the students' own beliefs. By plumbing the logic of another person's opinions, readers will be better able to assess their own thinking. And this, in turn, can promote the type of introspection that leads to a conviction based on reason. Though *Contemporary Issues* offers the opportunity to shape one's own opinions in light of competing or concordant philosophies, above all, it shows readers that well-reasoned, well-intentioned arguments can be countered by opposing opinions of equal worth.

Critically examining one's own opinions as well as the opinions of others is what Walter Lippmann believes makes an individual "civilized." Developing the skill early can only aid a reader's understanding of both moral conviction and political action. For students, a facility for reasoning is indispensable. Comprehending the foundations of opinions leads the student to the heart of controversy—to a recognition of what is at stake when holding a certain viewpoint. But the goal is not detached analysis; the issues are often far too immediate for that. The *Contemporary Issues* series induces the reader not only to see the shape of a current controversy, but to engage it, to respond to it, and ultimately to find one's place within it.

Introduction ■

Down a Slippery Slope?

A RTHUR CAPLAN IS A SPECIALIST in answering the tough questions of medicine—not the technological ones, relating to what *can* be done, but the moral ones, relating to what *should* be done. Caplan became interested in these kinds of medical issues because of his own experience. In 1996 he explained to a *New York Times Magazine* interviewer,

> When I was 7, I had polio. . . . That definitely got me interested in ethics. . . . I thought about things like why the hospital didn't let your parents stay over. I wondered about why such a bad thing had happened to me since I was such a good kid. Truthfulness bothered me a lot. The doctors and nurses . . . would never tell you when a kid was going to die.[1]

Caplan has never forgotten that lonely child in the hospital bed, but he has come a long way since then. Today, as head of the University of Pennsylvania's Center for Bioethics, he considers difficult medical issues from the standpoint not only of patients but of doctors, hospitals, health care planners, and society as a whole. He told the interviewer,

> I spend a lot of time trying to identify ethical issues in health care and science and then thinking through ways of arguing about them to change behavior. Or policy. Or both.[2]

Caplan's specialty of bioethics, or biomedical ethics, applies the basic principles of ethics—good and evil, right and wrong—to issues in medical research and health care. These issues more than just concern philosophers like Caplan. Especially in developed countries like the

9

United States, more people are using more health care services than ever before. Sooner or later, everyone needs health care, and one way or another, everyone pays for it. Questions about how medical care is developed and delivered therefore worry most citizens. More and more often, the troubling ethical side of medical issues makes newspaper headlines and causes spirited, often angry, public debate. "People are in the grip of bioethics fever,"[3] Caplan says.

Sliding Down a Slippery Slope

Some of the most thorny issues in bioethics today arise because people are aware that actions can have meaning beyond themselves. Taking one action, or accepting an action as ethically sound, can make taking or accepting a second action easier, even though that second action might be less defensible than the first.

For this reason, many bioethicists, and ordinary citizens as well, see certain issues in medical ethics as "slippery slopes." At the top of each slope are actions that seem to present little or no ethical problem in themselves, such as treating hereditary diseases by

A nurse assists an elderly hospice patient. As the demand for health care rises, ethical questions about its distribution are brought to the public's attention.

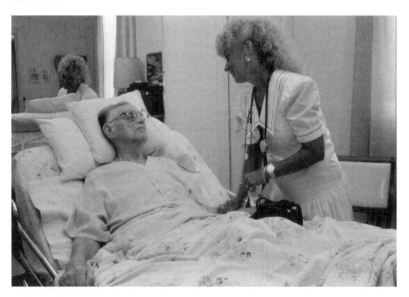

replacing defective genes. However, some people question the ethics of these actions because they fear that accepting them will lead to acceptance of more ethically doubtful actions, such as changing genes merely to improve a child's appearance. Accepting these questionable actions, in turn, might lead to actions that most people would find unethical, such as changing genes in order to give one group power over another group or to eliminate certain ethnic groups entirely. These actions are at the bottom of the slope.

Will accepting the actions at the top of an ethical slippery slope really lead to accepting those at the bottom? If not, at what point on the slope does a slide to the bottom become unavoidable? Where on the slope should one draw the line between ethical and unethical actions?

Naturally, people's opinions on these points differ. Even actions at the top of each slope have their critics, and actions near the bottom have their defenders. Deciding where to draw the line on issues that present a slippery slope is one of the biggest challenges that bioethicists and concerned citizens face today.

Conflicting Values

One of the reasons that drawing the line on slippery slope issues is so hard is that different people may judge these issues in terms of different values. If several values are involved in an issue, people may have different feelings about which value is most important. The value they choose will affect where they draw the line on the slope.

The principles or values that bioethicists apply to medical issues are the same ones applied to other issues in ethics. In most modern Western cultures, the most important values are probably these six, defined by Kathy A. Fackelmann in *Science News:*

Autonomy—being free to make decisions involving one's own or a family member's health and well-being.

Beneficence—doing the right thing; providing or promoting well-being and preventing harm.

Justice—being fair.

Nonmaleficence—doing no harm; acting with no harmful or selfish motives toward another person or society.

Veracity—telling the truth.

Fidelity—keeping all contracts and promises.[4]

Ethical problems arise when two or more values suggest conflicting actions or conflicting judgments about a particular action. This happens often in modern medicine. For instance, desperately ill people sometimes ask their doctors for drugs to use to commit suicide. Doctors who place a high value on the principle of autonomy might see providing such drugs as ethical because it shows respect for patients' decisions about their own lives. Doctors who value nonmaleficence above autonomy, on the other hand, might refuse to aid in harming a person, even though the person wishes it.

New Technology, New Questions

Individuals have always had to make choices between conflicting values. Today, however, choices in bioethics are complicated by the rapid advances that have occurred in medical technology. Perhaps it is not surprising that bioethics became a major field only about twenty years ago, when technologies such as organ transplantation

Dr. Jack Kevorkian poses with Marcella Lawrence (left) and Marguerit Tate (right) following a press conference about a bill that bans assisted suicide. Both women later took their lives with Kevorkian's assistance.

began to revolutionize medicine. Those same new technologies have revolutionized medical ethics, redefining old slippery slopes and creating new ones. This trend is likely to grow even more in the future. Ethicist Joseph Fletcher explains,

> As medicine's achievements proliferate, and as its control of life, health, and death increases, the frequency, complexity, and subtlety of its decision making also necessarily increase.[5]

For example, machines can now maintain a person's breathing and heartbeat after these bodily functions normally would have stopped. The invention of these machines forced doctors and lawmakers to redefine death. During the 1970s, after much discussion, they changed the clinical definition of death from "when the heart stops beating" to "when the brain stops functioning." This in turn changed the legal and ethical view of actions such as removing a beating heart from a person's body, as transplant surgeons may do with people who are "brain dead." Many people now find such an action ethically acceptable under these circumstances, even though formerly it would have been seen as murder.

More and more people are questioning whether medical developments that are technologically possible are also ethically right. The fact that technology can preserve some degree of life almost indefinitely has raised new questions about what "natural death" is and when it should be permitted, or perhaps even helped, to occur. Because new medical technology is very expensive and some resources it uses, such as donor organs, are in short supply, giving a person all the medical care that might be technologically possible may not be ethical because doing so would deprive others of needed care. Technology is also increasingly becoming able to change human genes, which raises questions about which changes are ethical to make. The process of creating new technologies brings up still other ethical questions, such as what cost in the lives of animals is justified to perfect new drugs or increase the supply of transplantable organs.

None of these bioethical questions raised by new technology has a simple yes-or-no answer. Rather, each requires decisions about

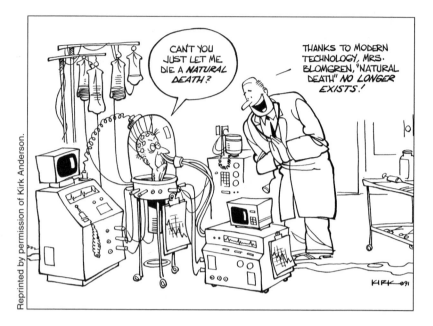

Reprinted by permission of Kirk Anderson.

a wide range of possible actions. Many people see such actions arranged on a slippery slope.

New Decision Makers

Medical issues are also more complicated than they used to be because the process of making decisions about health care and medical research is changing. Physicians, or medical doctors, used to make most decisions about how health care was used; scientists made most decisions about how research was done. Today, however, members of the public are demanding a larger share in decision making, both for themselves as individuals and for their communities. Letters to legislators and newspapers show that many people have strong opinions about ethical issues in medical care and research, and they want a voice in deciding those issues.

Even more important, both professionals (doctors and scientists) and the public are increasingly elbowed aside in the decision-making process by the "third parties" who pay for health care and research. People used to pay doctors or other health care professionals directly for each service performed. Today, however, most health care comes through government programs, private insurance, or managed health care organizations. (Managed health care organizations both pay for and provide health care services for their members.) The administrators of these programs and organizations affect many health care decisions by making rules about what they will—and will not—pay for. Similarly, government and large businesses provide much of the money that now pays for medical research. This means that politicians and businesspeople, rather than scientists, often determine what research is done and how. All these third-party groups have interests, such as saving or making money, that may differ from those of doctors, scientists, and the public. The result is more conflicts in health care and research decisions and more disagreements about where certain actions fall on the slippery slope between ethical and unethical.

"Ethics won't allow us to pull the plug until he runs out of money."

Many bioethicists agree that the greatest danger in medical ethics today comes from the fact that decisions about vital medical issues are often made secretly, without input from everyone concerned. When debate is open, opponents often use name-calling and inflammatory language rather than reasoning to support their opinions. As long as these things are true, there is little chance to make health care and research decisions calmly, logically, and with understanding and respect for differences. If society is ever to reach a consensus on these knotty and often frightening bioethical questions—to decide where to put a stop sign on each slippery slope—public discussion that is both open and rational must take place.

Chapter 1

How Should Health Care Be Allocated?

IN 1993, TWIN BABY GIRLS were born to a Pennsylvania family named Lakeberg. The two girls' bodies were joined, and they shared a heart and a liver. The twins' parents demanded that surgeons try to separate the girls, even though they were told that one girl would surely die during the operation and there was a less than 1 percent chance that the other would survive the surgery. The operation took place, and baby Amy died. Angela, the other twin, lived for a year before she, too, passed away. The cost of the futile attempt to save these two babies was $1.3 million.

A growing number of people would say that this money was wasted. They would point out that it could have been used to save the lives of other children who were not so sick. Alternatively, it could have provided prenatal (before birth) care, thereby increasing the number of mothers who bear babies that are not sick at all. Some people have begun demanding that such expensive and seemingly hopeless medical rescue efforts be limited. Ethicist B. D. Cohen asks, for instance,

> Do we really want to [spend more than $2 billion a year] saving pound-and-a-half babies [those born very prematurely, who have an extremely low chance of survival] in an era when we are cutting back on childhood immunization and school lunch programs? Should we be spending an average of $140,000 per baby for neonatal [newborn] intensive care when about 15 percent of the survivors will suffer from defects of one kind or another? These are easy questions to duck. They are not easy questions to answer.[6]

17

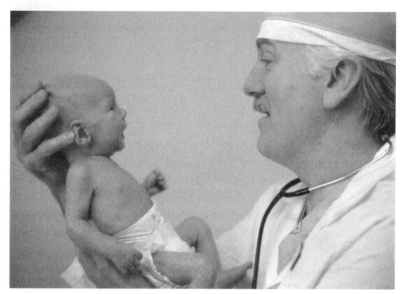

A physician examines a heart transplant baby. Many people question the value of techniques used to prolong the lives of babies who have a very poor chance of survival.

Babies like Rebecca Cataldo make such questions even harder to answer. Rebecca, born in 1990 after only twenty-four weeks in her mother's womb instead of the usual thirty-eight weeks, was one of the "pound-and-a-half babies" that Cohen talks about. In fact, she weighed less than that—barely over a pound. At birth, her chances of survival were hardly better than Amy's and Angela's.

Rebecca spent three-and-a-half months on a respirator that breathed for her, undergoing treatment that cost as much as $2,000 a day. Without that treatment, she would have died. With it, however, she not only survived but grew into a healthy child. Would it have been ethical to limit the amount of money spent to save this little girl's life? Not surprisingly, Rebecca's mother, Mary, thinks not. "I don't get this cutoff thing,"[7] she told an interviewer in 1994.

Rising Health Costs: A Need for Limits?

Many Americans would like to duck questions about limits on health care. They find it hard to accept the idea that anyone—especially themselves—should be denied any kind of care that they need or want. As

Harriet Washington wrote in *Emerge* magazine in 1994, "Americans view state-of-the-art, high-technology health care as a right, not a privilege."[8] In a *Newsweek* poll taken in the same year, 78 percent of the people polled said they would not accept fewer choices of doctors or hospitals, even if doing so would bring down costs and help to guarantee basic health care coverage for everyone. Sixty percent were unwilling to limit their possible use of medical specialists or technology.

Limiting or rationing health care seems not only undesirable but unethical to many. It appears to violate American ideals of equality, justice, and autonomy. Daniel Callahan, president of New York's Hastings Center for bioethics research, explains that Americans' dislike of health care rationing

> expresses . . . some of our most admired values . . . our touching faith in the power of efficiency, our commitment to egalitarianism, and our reluctance officially to pick upon the poor to test our social schemes.[9]

A need for limits on health care, however, is becoming harder to deny because health care costs are rising so fast. In 1994, according to an article in the *New England Journal of Medicine,* people in the United States spent over 14 percent of the gross domestic product (GDP)—the combined value of all the goods and services made in the country—on health care. Health care costs are rising much faster than other costs, so their percentage of the GDP keeps growing. Money spent on health care cannot be spent on other things, such as education or housing. Furthermore, all of that money comes out of citizens' pockets in one form or another. Health care paid for by private insurance or government programs may seem free, but it affects insurance premiums and taxes.

Several reasons have been offered to explain why the cost of health care has risen so far and so fast. One reason is that health care has sometimes been provided inefficiently or wastefully. Fearing lawsuits or giving in to patients' demands, doctors sometimes order tests or treatments that are not really useful. Critics also claim that some health care providers charge too much for their services. Doctors, hospitals, insurance companies, and makers of drugs and other medical treatments have all been accused of making excess profits.

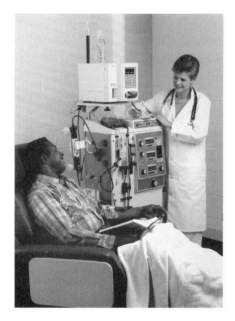

A man undergoes hemodialysis treatment to cleanse his blood of poisonous waste products that his kidneys are no longer able to remove.

Progress has been made in controlling inefficiency, waste, and excess profits since the mid-1980s, when large numbers of Americans first became concerned about rising health care costs. Still, most health care policy analysts agree that more in this area can and should be done. A few, such as Lawrence D. Brown, think that "budgeting, planning, regulation, and negotiation" [10] aimed at reducing waste will be enough to solve the health care cost crisis. Many, however, do not. Health care policy analyst and former Colorado governor Richard Lamm writes,

> Even if we could successfully remove all the inefficiencies from the American medical system, we are still confronted by a new painful reality: Infinite medical needs have run into finite resources. [11]

High-technology medicine and growing demands for health care have also come in for shares of the blame for rising costs. New technology seems miraculous, but its price tag is high: about $150,000 to transplant a heart or save a premature baby, for instance. "We have invented more medicine than we can pay for," [12] says Richard Lamm. Still more important, says David Eddy, a physician who advocates controlling health care costs, is the fact that "Each year we [health care providers] do more to the average patient."[13] As more of the American population reaches old age and more types of new technology become available, use of health care services is likely to increase still more.

Medical Standards: "When in Doubt, Don't"

Rising health care demands and costs are slowly forcing Americans to face the fact that, sooner or later, some health care probably will have to be denied to some people who need or want it. But how will this be done, by whom, and according to what standards? Health care rationing may start off as a sensible attempt to reduce waste, control costs, and make sure that everyone has basic care. Many people fear, however, that once begun, rationing plans will slide farther and farther down a slippery ethical slope until they end up sacrificing lives simply to save—or make—money.

Most people would say that the most acceptable standards for judging what health care will be given to which patients are medical

Doctors work to transplant a heart. Such lifesaving treatment is enormously expensive, and many wonder if health care efforts such as these should be limited.

ones, and that the best people to make those judgments are doctors. Since medicine's beginning, doctors' first duty has been to do what is best for their patients. Yet thoughtful doctors have always recognized that "doing what is best" sometimes means saying no. Most doctors, for instance, would not try to obtain a heart transplant for someone who is eighty years old or has advanced cancer. They might not try to prolong the life of someone who is permanently unconscious or in great pain.

At its best, health care rationing might simply mean that doctors would need to make the same kinds of judgments they have always made but make them more carefully. David Eddy recommends following the principle of "When in doubt, don't."[14] In other words, doctors should not recommend treatments that have only a small chance of success or tests that have only a small chance of finding disease in a particular person. If several tests or treatments are likely to work equally well, doctors should choose the least expensive one.

Eddy feels that most health care rationing can be handled through these kinds of decisions. He says they can lead not only to saving money but to improving medical care.

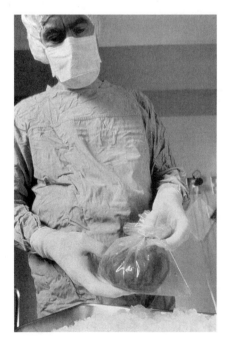

A surgeon holds a donated kidney, ready to be transplanted. The number of people in need of such organs far exceeds the supply.

Many high-value practices [treatments and tests that have proven high medical benefit to patients] are underused, and many low-value practices are overused. . . . The strategy is to trade resources from . . . overused low-value practices to the underused high-value practices. . . . Every time we [doctors] . . . [do this], we will simultaneously increase quality and reduce costs.[15]

A problem with medical standards for rationing, though, is that most such standards are difficult—perhaps impossible—for even highly trained and experienced physicians to define or measure exactly. Such terms as *benefit, quality of life,* and *medical need* can have very different meanings to different doctors and different patients. "It has turned out to be impossible to specify a purely scientific standard of medical need,"[16] writes Daniel Callahan.

Sometimes it is also hard to know which of several conflicting medical standards to apply. For instance, who should be the first to receive scarce organs for transplantation: the sickest people, who need them the most, or healthier people, who are more likely to survive and benefit from the transplants? The United Network for Organ Sharing (UNOS), which oversees all organ transplants in the United States, reversed its policy on this point, at least in regard to liver transplants, in 1996. Formerly, the transplants went first to the patients who were sickest. Now, however, explains Richard Thistlethwaite, chief transplantation surgeon at the University of Chicago, "The decision has been made to say, 'Let's ration [livers] to the ones with the greatest chance of being helped.'"[17]

Guidelines: Does One "Size" Really Fit All?

The difficulty of rationing health care according to medical standards grows greater when people who are not doctors or are not familiar with particular patients intrude on the decision-making process. Today this happens more and more often because a growing number of doctors either work for managed health care organizations or treat patients who belong to such organizations. These organizations often formalize medical standards into written guidelines. They more or less force the doctors and hospitals that they

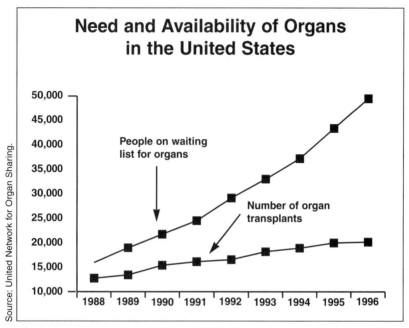

Need and Availability of Organs in the United States

Source: United Network for Organ Sharing.

People on waiting list for organs

Number of organ transplants

employ or buy services from to follow these guidelines when prescribing tests and treatments.

Government health care plans also may use guidelines to ration health care. In 1993, for example, voters in the state of Oregon approved a system in which about seven hundred medical treatments were ranked in order of importance to overall health. The state, which contributed funds to Medicaid, the state and federal government program that pays for medical care for the poor, said it would not pay for the hundred or so treatments at the bottom of the list.

The main problem with guidelines is that they do not make allowances for patients whose situation differs from the average. For instance, young women seldom get breast cancer, and several research studies have found that mammograms (breast X rays) detect very few cases of cancer in women under fifty. Some managed care organizations' guidelines therefore exclude mammograms for women in this age group. Women who have several family members with breast cancer, however, are much more likely than average to develop breast tumors at an early age. The mammograms that might be a waste of money for most young women could be lifesavers for these few, yet the guidelines deny the tests to them as well as others.

Because guidelines leave little room for doctors to use their judgment in meeting individual patients' needs, critics say, they are likely to make medical care less effective. William Schwartz, a medical professor at Tufts University, says, "The expected value or payoff from any [medical] procedure depends on the particular characteristics and severity of an illness in a *particular patient.*" [18]

In addition to guidelines, some managed care organizations place a further limit on doctors' freedom to choose care for their patients. Doctors' decisions are reviewed, and can be reversed, by health plan administrators who see patients' medical records but never meet the patients themselves. Such reviewers may miss subtle clues about a patient's health that the person's own doctor, who often has known him or her for years, can pick up. One former health plan reviewer, Linda Peeno, said that the distance between herself and patients, who were just names on a computer screen to her, made it easier to deny treatments, "like bomber pilots in war who never see the faces of their victims." [19]

A woman undergoes a mammogram to diagnose whether she may have breast cancer. Some health care providers restrict the use of such tests in young women.

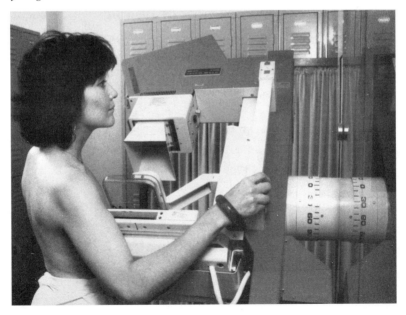

A reviewer also may not know or care about the personal and social effects of giving or denying a particular treatment. In a 1996 issue of the *New England Journal of Medicine*, for example, cancer specialists Brent Weston and Marie Lauria described a child with leukemia (a blood cancer) whom health care plan reviewers forced to go out of state for a bone marrow transplant, even though hospitals closer to where the child lived could have performed the treatment equally well. Weston and Lauria, his doctors, protested the reviewers' decision, but their objections were ignored. The time and money spent on this extra travel eventually cost the child's parents their jobs, savings, and home.

In spite of such horror stories, health plan managers insist that reviewers' judgments are usually valid. The California Association of Health Plans told a state Assembly committee,

> Many sound, safe medical decisions have been made and are made daily based on the medical records of the patient . . . and the medical literature on the proposed treatment. Examination of the patient would rarely change the scientific basis for performing a procedure.[20]

Lifestyle Judgments: Medical or Moral?

Some standards for health care rationing seem to be medical but, at least in part, are really judgments of social or moral worth. Therefore, many doctors and others find them more ethically questionable—farther down the slippery slope—than standards that are strictly medical.

One such standard is based on a patient's lifestyle, the everyday choices that the person makes about how to behave. Aspects of lifestyle, such as diet, smoking habits, and sexual behavior, certainly can affect health and the probable outcome of medical treatments. Denying treatment on the basis of lifestyle, however, seems to critics to be as much a punishment for behavior that society deems "bad" as it is a medical judgment.

On the one hand, some say that people whose lifestyles helped to cause their illnesses should not receive scarce health care resources. For example, they believe that alcoholics whose drinking

Excessive smoking and drinking are two behaviors that result in many health care complications. Should people who make such damaging lifestyle choices be allowed to command the same access to expensive health care treatments as those who do not?

has ruined their livers should be denied liver transplants. Supporters of this approach say that in return for the privilege of health care paid for at least in part by society (through taxes or insurance premiums), people owe society an effort to keep themselves from getting sick. "People simply will not want to have their premiums or taxes increased to pay for the *avoidable afflictions* of others,"[21] points out James Childress, professor of medicine and religious studies at the University of Virginia, although he himself does not support this standard of rationing.

Critics of using lifestyle as a standard for health care rationing say that doing so is an infringement on patients' autonomy and liberty. "The principle of liberty sets a presumption against governmental interference in matters of lifestyle and voluntary risk-taking,"[22] Childress believes. Furthermore, he notes, definitions of a "healthy" lifestyle can vary just as much as other judgments of an individual's social or moral worth. "The danger is that . . . a certain style of life will be enforced in the name of health although it has little to do with health and more to do with the legislation of morality"[23]—morality as defined by some particular group.

Social Standards: Treatment for One or Many?

Many people would say that applying strictly social standards to health care rationing is less ethical than using standards that are at least partly medical. Some types of social standards may have a legitimate place in deciding how health care will be distributed, however. Some ethicists, for instance, say that the emphasis in American health care should be changed from individuals to populations. Richard Lamm believes that

> public funds should buy the most health for the most people. . . . We must recognize that the ultimate ethical question is not how to give all the "beneficial" medicine to each individual but how to maximize the health of the community.[24]

Health care analysts who favor this emphasis on populations say that doctors who work for managed care organizations need to focus less on the needs of the patients they see personally and more on the needs of all the people that the organization serves. David Eddy says, "When physicians hoard resources for their own patients, they are not taking from [health plan] administrators or insurers; they are taking from other patients."[25]

Emphasizing the needs of groups over those of individuals appeals to the values of justice and equality, but it may be a hard approach to sell to the American public. A focus on individuals is a major part of mainstream Western culture, especially in the United States. Furthermore, James Childress points out,

> Decisions to try to rescue identified individuals have symbolic value. . . . [They] show that individuals are "priceless" and that society is "too good" to let them die without great efforts to save them. This is society's myth.[26]

The myth is reinforced by media stories and programs that emphasize the needs of individuals, such as TV telethons that feature appearances by sick children. Such programs help people forget that seemingly anonymous groups are also made up of suffering individuals. As Leslie S. Rothenberg, a professor of medicine and an ethicist, asks,

Is the human tragedy and the personal anguish of death [for an individual] from the lack of an organ transplant any greater than that of an infant dying in an intensive-care unit from a preventable problem brought about by lack of prenatal care?[27]

Those who suggest changing the emphasis of health care from individuals to populations also often ask for a change in emphasis from "rescue medicine," which treats disease after it develops, to preventive medicine, which tries to keep people from becoming sick in the first place. The two changes are related. Preventive medicine, such as vaccination and prenatal care programs, is usually applied to large groups, whereas rescue medicine is applied to individuals.

Preventive care is usually less expensive than rescue medicine, so a given amount of money spent on prevention can reach more

Kimberly Fuller, seventeen, poses with her mother at Children's Hospital in Pittsburgh. Fuller received transplanted lungs which her body is rejecting. The family hopes that Kimberly will have a chance for a second set of lungs. Ethicists debate whether one individual has a "right" to such a second chance when so many others are waiting.

people than the same amount spent on rescue care. On the other hand, the effects of preventive care are not as easy to identify as those of rescue medicine. Although he generally supports a switch to more preventive medicine, James Childress says,

> The evidence for the effectiveness and efficiency of a preventive strategy to reduce morbidity [disease] and premature mortality [early death] . . . is by no means conclusive.[28]

Hidden Standards: Lack of Money and Access

Not everyone believes that health care rationing according to the social standard of the good of the group is ethical. Most people would say, however, that some other social standards that affect health care rationing are even less morally acceptable. These standards are seldom applied formally, yet they effectively limit health care for some people. Such standards may penalize people for lack of money, transportation, or understanding of a language or bureaucratic system.

Secret or *de facto* health care rationing exists in many forms. Ethicist Steven A. Schroeder writes,

> Implicit [unstated] rationing can be carried out . . . by budget, as when . . . health plans limit [the amount of] certain services; by price, when services such as cosmetic surgery are not covered by health insurance; by queue [line], when certain services are not immediately available; by hassle, when administrative barriers facing physicians and patients deter [block] the delivery of services; by insurance coverage; and by subtle social factors.[29]

Whether health care providers and program managers admit it or not, a patient's income has always played a part in rationing decisions. Wealth allows people to buy treatments not covered by insurance or other programs, for instance. Money also partly governs access to organ transplant waiting lists, because people must show that they can pay transplant-related costs, either on their own or through insurance, before being put on a list. "The effect one's ability to pay has in securing access to transplantation makes the current method of distributing organs morally suspect,"[30] says Arthur Caplan.

The injustice of rationing health care according to ability to pay is obvious, yet it is a part of the capitalist system that most Americans support. Even if a national health care system eventually guarantees basic care to all, those who can pay for treatments not covered by the system probably will continue to get better care than those who cannot. Not everyone sees this as wrong. As Richard Lamm puts it, "We give food stamps, but we don't give people the right to go to Jack's [an expensive restaurant] for dinner."[31] Some ethicists say, however, that if a medical treatment is denied to some people for cost reasons, it should be denied to all.

Ironically, the very poor sometimes have a financial advantage in getting health care. They may have access to government programs denied to the working poor, who have too high an income to qualify for these programs but are not covered by health insurance at work and cannot afford to buy it on their own. However, government health programs are also often the first to suffer rationing, as happened in Oregon. "Rationing is a special danger to the poor and minority-group members,"[32] writes Harriet Washington.

Rationing has been done unofficially on the basis of access as well as income. Sometimes access is a matter of location. In some inner-city and rural areas, for instance, few doctors or hospitals exist, and people who live in these areas often lack easy transportation to better-equipped places. Such people, therefore, may have trouble getting health care. Location also plays a role in assigning organ transplants because UNOS divides the country into eleven regions with separate waiting lists. More organs are donated in some regions than others, and UNOS rarely ships organs outside the region where they are donated.

Access is sometimes limited in more subtle ways as well. People with little education or ability to speak English may not know how or whom to ask for the care they need. People who do not have a regular doctor to give them basic or primary care may also lack access to specialized treatments because primary-care doctors are usually the ones who send patients to specialists. A person's primary-care doctor must put him or her on a transplant waiting list, for instance.

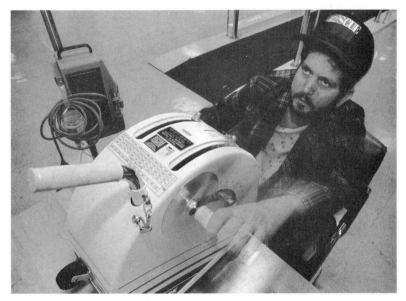

*A man uses a machine to keep fit while waiting for an intestine
transplant. Some people believe that access to lifesaving transplants
depends too much on income and location.*

Profit-Making Standards: Dying to Make Money

Most doctors and patients would agree that the least desirable standards for health care rationing—those at the bottom of the slippery
slope—are standards based strictly on a desire to make money.
Today, more and more managed health care organizations are run
for profit. Their decisions about which treatments to fund, therefore,
may be based more on the desire to save or make money than on
medical standards. Former surgeon general C. Everett Koop writes,
"When profit, not health, is the objective, it poses a real threat to the
doctor-patient relationship."[33]

    Some profit-oriented health care plans offer doctors a financial
incentive to limit recommendations of expensive care. They may
give the doctors bonuses for keeping costs low or reduce the doctors' pay if costs go above a certain level. Such health plans "pit the
financial interests of the doctor against the interests of the patient,"
says Mark Barnes, executive director of the AIDS Action Council.
"That's a dangerous situation."[34]

This financial conflict of interest limits the autonomy of both doctor and patient. It is also likely to reduce people's trust in their doctors. The American Medical Association's Council on Ethical and Judicial Affairs insists that "physicians must place patients' interests ahead of their own interests, including financial remuneration [payment]."[35] But doctors are human, and not all will behave so nobly. How, critics ask, will a patient know which choices his or her doctor has made?

Stories about managed health care organizations that deny treatments seemingly without reason or provide poor treatment have given many people a bad image of these organizations. In a 1997 Harris poll, just 51 percent of the people polled said that managed health care organizations do a good job in serving consumers. By comparison, 83 percent said that physicians serve people well, and 79 percent said that drug companies, another popular target for critics of health care, do so.

Supporters of managed care cite other polls saying that 80 or 90 percent of people are satisfied with the care given by their health plans. These supporters say that criticism arises mostly because people do not fully understand how managed health plans work. They also say that the public's feelings are distorted by hearing about a

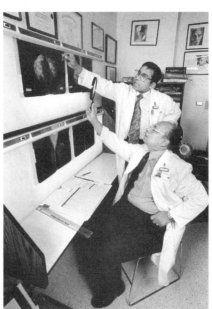

Radiologists examine the results of a mammogram that reveals a cancerous growth. Many ethicists wonder whether managed care organizations have a hidden incentive to deny patients expensive tests like this.

small number of badly managed cases, just as people may become afraid of flying after reading about a few spectacular air crashes. People forget the thousands of patients treated successfully every day, just as they forget the thousands of planes that land safely.

A more important cause of the widely differing opinions about managed care plans is the fact that not all such plans are alike. Carolyn M. Clancy and Howard Brody, writing in the *Journal of the American Medical Association,* see health plans in terms of the Robert Louis Stevenson story *Dr. Jekyll and Mr. Hyde.* In that story, the good Dr. Jekyll drinks a potion that turns him into the evil Mr. Hyde.

Clancy and Brody say that, among managed care programs, there are "Jekyll plans" at one extreme and "Hyde plans" at the other. A Jekyll plan

> encourages personal and long-standing relationships between the patient and the primary provider [family doctor], a commitment to caring for the same population of patients over time, and a[n] . . . approach to medical practice that incorporates public health as well as individual medical care strategies.[36]

Profits of Jekyll plans are invested in improvements in patient care. Hyde plans, by contrast,

> control costs by . . . exclusion of sicker patients, rationing by inconvenience, burdensome . . . [criticism] of clinical [medical] decisions, or denial of beneficial but expensive care to some patients.[37]

Profits in these plans are returned to stockholders. Clancy and Brody hope that in the future, physicians as a group will be able to pressure managed care organizations to increase the number of Jekyll plans and decrease the number of Hyde plans.

A Need for Discussion

Many ethicists say that the most important thing people can do to ensure that health care rationing will be done in the fairest possible way is to face the fact that rationing is necessary and discuss openly the standards and methods by which it should be done. Everyone involved should contribute to the discussion: program administrators, doctors and other health care providers, sick people or groups that represent them, and healthy members of the community. Ethicist Gregory Pence says,

> Medical costs are uncontrollable because we lack moral agreement about how to deny medical services. Deciding how to say "no," and to say it with honesty and integrity, is perhaps the most profound, most difficult moral question our society will face in coming years. But face it we must, for the alternative is disastrous.[38]

Chapter 2

Should Doctors Ever Hasten Patients' Deaths?

"PAIN EXCRUCIATING. CAN'T WALK,"[39] wrote thirty-nine-year-old Rebecca Badger on July 8, 1996. The next day, Badger gave herself a fatal injection of drugs with the aid of Jack Kevorkian, a retired Michigan pathologist (physician who specializes in the study of diseased tissue) who has staged a highly publicized crusade to make it legal for doctors to help people like Badger commit suicide. By early 1997, Kevorkian had personally helped forty-six people end their lives.

Eight years before, after hearing Badger describe her pain, difficulty in walking, and the tingling and numbness in her arms and legs, a doctor had told her that she probably had multiple sclerosis. This incurable disease slowly makes nerves degenerate. Badger's illness had worsened so much since that time that she sought death. Yet, when a medical examiner studied her body after she died, he found no sign of any physical ailment. "Looking backward and looking at the autopsy," Johanna Meyer-Mitchell, one of several doctors who had treated Badger, concluded, "this woman died of a psychiatric disease."[40]

Badger had a history of depression, alcoholism, and addiction to painkilling drugs. Her seemingly physical illness may have had a mental cause. It might have gone away if she had received treatment for depression instead of a lethal injection. Should she have been prevented from killing herself, or at least denied help in doing so, until such treatment had been tried? Or should she have had the right to decide whether her own life was worth living? If she did have that right, should she also have had the right to ask for skilled help in ending that life?

36

A Slippery Slope to Death

Troubling deaths like Rebecca Badger's have fueled an international debate over whether doctors should be allowed to help people end their lives or even to cause their deaths if they cannot do so themselves. "Few [other] issues are as personal and divisive,"[41] Joseph Shapiro noted in a 1994 *U.S. News & World Report* article. The ethical side of this issue has made headlines in the wake of Kevorkian's widely reported—and highly criticized—actions. The legal side of it has reached the U.S. Supreme Court.

Ironically, the demand for a so-called right to die has grown out of medical technology's awesome power to keep people alive. "Modern dying has become fearsome," Shapiro stated. "Doctors now possess the technology to forestall [postpone] natural death almost indefinitely."[42] Respirators, heart pacemakers, feeding tubes, and other devices can keep bodies functioning long after consciousness has permanently departed. They can keep death from ending the tremendous pain of diseases such as AIDS and cancer. Right-to-die supporters say that doctors, in their determination to preserve life, fail to take into account the quality of that life and the fact that patients or their families may not want it preserved.

Arguments over physician-assisted death pit powerful ethical duties against each other. On one side is the duty to preserve human life. On the other is the duty to respect individual liberty and autonomy. As with allocation of health care, many people see this issue as a

Dr. Jack Kevorkian, sometimes called "Doctor Death," is controversial for his role in helping critically ill patients take their own lives.

BY TOLES FOR THE BUFFALO NEWS

slippery slope. At the top is a desire to ease the agony of people who are already dying. At the bottom, some say, is what amounts to legalized murder.

Until this century, suicide was held to be morally wrong and legally criminal. The law no longer punishes people who try to kill themselves. Helping someone commit suicide, however, is still against the law in most states. But which medical actions that cause death should be punished under these laws? And should the laws themselves be changed? The answers are by no means clear.

Doctors can deliberately cause death in three ways. First, they can discontinue treatment that keeps a person alive. If a respirator is maintaining the person's breathing, for instance, they can turn the respirator off. Second, they can give a person the means to commit suicide, such as prescribing a lethal dose of painkilling pills. Third, they can cause a person's death directly by giving, say, a lethal injection. Society's opinion about which of these actions should be legally and morally permitted has been changing rapidly.

Three Tragedies

Today the law in most countries, including the United States, allows mentally competent adults to refuse medical treatment, even though doing so will cause their deaths. Most people, though not all, find this morally acceptable. If a person is not competent—in a permanent coma or "persistent vegetative state," for instance—a doctor may legally stop treatment on the basis of advance written directives left by the patient or of requests by the patient's family. Open acceptance of these actions is only a little more than twenty years old, however. It came about because of three highly publicized tragedies, all involving young women.

The first woman was Karen Ann Quinlan. One night in 1975, when she was just twenty-one years old, Quinlan took tranquilizer pills and later consumed a large amount of alcohol, not realizing that the two drugs made a deadly combination. She collapsed and went into a coma. After a few months, Quinlan's doctors told her parents that she probably would never wake up. The Quinlans said their daughter would not have wanted to live that way. They asked the doctors to "pull the plug" on the respirator that kept her alive.

The doctors refused, pointing out that they would break the law if they honored such a request. The Quinlans then went to court to get permission to have Karen's respirator turned off. The New Jersey Supreme Court granted them permission in March 1976. The judges ruled that the right of a patient or the patient's representatives to refuse medical treatment grows as the "degree of bodily invasion increases and the prognosis [prediction of medical outcome] dims."[43] Ironically, Karen Quinlan began breathing on her own after her respirator was disconnected. She lived almost ten more years, though she never became conscious again.

Nancy Cruzan was the second young woman to make medical and legal history. An automobile accident in 1983 left Cruzan in a permanent coma much like Quinlan's. Cruzan's parents, too, believed that their child would have wanted her life ended under these conditions. No one could recall Cruzan having made a clear statement to that effect, however.

Unlike Quinlan, Cruzan did not need a respirator, so there was no plug to pull. Cruzan's parents asked her doctors to remove the tubes that carried food and water into her body so that she would die. To some people, this seemed significantly different from turning off a respirator that sustained life artificially. To others, it did not.

Cruzan's parents, like Quinlan's, had to fight a court battle. When the U.S. Supreme Court finally heard their case in 1990, they both lost and won. The court ruled that Cruzan's tubes could not be removed because there was too little evidence that she would have wanted this done. In general, however, the court held that competent adults have a "constitutionally protected liberty interest in refusing unwanted medical treatment,"[44] including lifesaving treatment. In the same year, Congress confirmed the right to refuse medical care in a federal law called the Patient Self-Determination Act.

Elizabeth Bouvia, a cerebral palsy victim since birth, asked to be allowed to die. The California Supreme Court agreed that she had the right to refuse lifesaving treatments.

A third woman brought up ethical questions even more disturbing than those surrounding Karen Quinlan and Nancy Cruzan. Elizabeth Bouvia was conscious, not in great pain, and not suffering from a fatal illness. An incurable brain disorder called cerebral palsy, however, made her body essentially useless from the neck down. (Most people with cerebral palsy are not so severely disabled.) In 1984, at age twenty-six, Bouvia asked her doctors to remove her food and water tubes and let her starve to death. The California Supreme Court ruled that she had the right to kill herself by refusing medical treatment. Interestingly, once Bouvia gained legal permission to order her tubes removed, she changed her mind about doing so.

Should Doctors Help People Die?

What about people who are just as hopelessly ill as Karen Quinlan, Nancy Cruzan, and Elizabeth Bouvia but do not need life support? They may wish to end their lives but lack the strength or the means to do so. Should they be allowed to ask their doctors to help them bring a quick, painless end to their misery? This is the point on the slippery slope of physician-assisted death where the most intense debate rages today. Most of the debate concerns physician-assisted suicide, in which a doctor provides the means but the patient consciously performs the action that ends life.

Supporters say that physician-assisted suicide—at least for terminally ill people (those expected to die within six months)—is, like refusal of medical treatment, becoming widely accepted in American society. They offer evidence such as a Gallup poll taken in April 1996, in which 75 percent of the people questioned said that doctors should be allowed to end the lives of the terminally ill if the patients wanted it. Other polls have suggested that over half the doctors in the United States want physician-assisted suicide made legal.

Critics say that polls are often flawed. For example, the people who respond to the polls may not make up a fair sample of a larger population. Furthermore, the critics point out, what people say is not always what they do, particularly at the ballot box. They point to the fact that measures that would have legalized physician-assisted suicide under some circumstances failed to win voter approval in

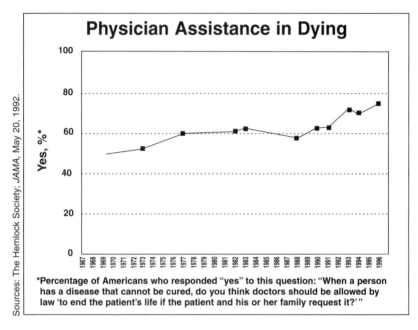

Sources: The Hemlock Society; JAMA, May 20, 1992.

Physician Assistance in Dying

*Percentage of Americans who responded "yes" to this question: "When a person has a disease that cannot be cured, do you think doctors should be allowed by law 'to end the patient's life if the patient and his or her family request it?'"

Washington and California in the early 1990s. A similar measure was passed in Oregon in 1994, however. In all three states, the vote was close. People's votes may have reflected feelings about the exact wording of the proposed laws and the safeguards they provided as much as, or more than, feelings about physician-assisted suicide itself.

The Liberty to Die

Laws both permitting and prohibiting physician-assisted suicide have been challenged in court. Groups who oppose the new Oregon law obtained a restraining order that has kept it from going into effect. (It will be placed on the state ballot for another vote in November 1997.) Meanwhile, other groups challenged laws that blocked physician-assisted suicide in Washington and New York. They won victories in federal circuit courts of appeals, which rule on cases throughout a region of the country. Opponents, in turn, challenged the appeals courts' rulings.

Barbara Dority of the Hemlock Society, a group that supports assisted suicide, says that "the right to die with dignity, in our own time and on our own terms [is] the ultimate civil right."[45] Judges in both circuit courts found support for that right within the Fourteenth Amendment to the U.S. Constitution. The two courts, however, referred to different parts of the amendment and used different logic to reach their conclusions.

The Ninth Circuit Court, which ruled on the Washington case, based its thinking on a parallel with abortion, which the U.S. Supreme Court had legalized in its famous *Roe v. Wade* decision of 1973. The Fourteenth Amendment says that no one can be deprived of life, liberty, or property without due process of law. In the *Roe* decision, the Supreme Court interpreted this to mean that people could not be forced to have their privacy or their bodies invaded without legal process. The high Court saw protection of these things as part of the protection of liberty. It said that the decision to have an abortion was a private matter in which the states should not interfere.

Ninth Circuit Court Judge Stephen Reinhardt ruled that the decision to ask a doctor for help in ending one's life is equally private and protected. He wrote that there is a "liberty interest in choosing the time and manner of one's own death."[46] Being able to make this decision freely is "central to personal dignity and autonomy."[47]

Ethically as well as legally, many people find the appeal to liberty and autonomy a powerful one. Mainstream American culture values individual freedom very highly. Marcia Angell, executive editor of the *New England Journal of Medicine,* calls autonomy "one of the most important ethical principles in medicine"[48] and says that when this principle conflicts with others in medical decision making, it should almost always come first.

Opponents of physician-assisted suicide, however, point out that autonomy has moral and legal limits. Legal theorists Robert P. George and William C. Porth Jr. write, "People possess a dignity to which rights attach that not even they have the moral authority to waive [give up], i.e. [that is], *inalienable* rights."[49] One of these inalienable rights is the right to life. The government, critics like these say, has an interest in preserving life even when the people whose lives are in question do not want them preserved.

Equal Rights to Death

The Second Circuit Court, whose region includes New York, used different reasoning to strike down that state's law against physician-assisted suicide. It focused on the part of the Fourteenth Amendment

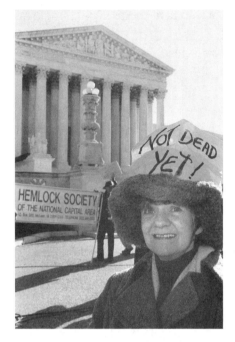

Demonstrators outside the Supreme Court protest physician-assisted suicide. Opponents believe that giving a person a lethal prescription to be used in suicide is the equivalent of murder.

that guarantees equal protection to all citizens. The judges saw no difference between withdrawing medical treatment and providing a lethal prescription at a patient's request; both, to them, were assisted suicide. Judge Roger Miner, expressing the court's majority opinion, wrote, "Physicians do not fulfill the role of 'killers' by prescribing drugs to hasten death any more than they do by disconnecting life-support systems."[50] Sick people who were not receiving life-supporting medical treatment, the judges said, deserved the same protection of the right to ask for death that had been granted to those who were receiving such treatment.

Opponents of physician-assisted suicide, however, see an important difference between the two actions. In withdrawing medical treatment, they say, a doctor is simply allowing natural death to occur. In providing a lethal prescription, however, the doctor is deliberately causing death. Acting Solicitor General Walter Dellinger has expressed the opposition to physician-assisted suicide of President Bill Clinton's administration by saying that there is "a common-sense distinction . . . between killing someone and letting them die."[51]

In 1997, arguments on the Washington and New York cases took the final judicial step: They reached the U.S. Supreme Court. On January 8 the Court agreed to hear both cases and determine whether laws against physician-assisted suicide are permitted by the Constitution. It rendered a unanimous decision on June 26, stating that no constitutionally protected right to die exists. In rejecting the appeals courts' rulings, the Supreme Court returned to the states the power to decide whether or not to permit physician-assisted suicide. Chief Justice William Rehnquist wrote,

> Throughout the nation, Americans are engaged in an earnest and profound debate about the morality, legality and practicality of physician-assisted suicide. Our holding [ruling] permits this debate to continue, as it should in a democratic society.[52]

Deadly Doctors

Physician-assisted suicide involves some ethical issues that the courts have not discussed. One is the change that assisted suicide might bring to doctors' and patients' understanding of the physician's job.

A demonstrator proclaims her position in favor of physician-assisted suicide. Proponents believe that people have the right to decide when to die, especially if they are terminally ill or in severe pain.

Physicians still begin their careers by taking the Hippocratic oath, which has been a central guideline for Western medical ethics since it was created in Greece about twenty-five hundred years ago. The oath contains the words, "I will neither give a deadly drug . . . if asked for it, nor will I make a suggestion to this effect."[53] Critics say that allowing physicians to kill, even with their patients' consent, violates the profession's focus on healing. The American Medical Association opposes physician-assisted suicide mostly for this reason.

If patients know that their doctors have the legal power to kill them, opponents of assisted suicide say, they might cease to trust the doctors. This apparently happened in the state of Northern Australia, which until recently was the only place in the world where physician-assisted suicide was legal. (The state passed a law permitting assisted suicide in July 1996 and repealed it in March 1997.) Opponents of the Australian law said it made some Aborigines, Australia's native people, afraid to seek medical care because they feared that doctors would kill them. Like native people in some other countries, the Aborigines had often been abused in the past, so their distrust was understandable. Critics say that poor, elderly, nonwhite, or other marginalized people in the United States might develop similar fears.

Marcia Angell writes, however,

> Contrary to the frequent assertions that permitting physician-assisted suicide would lead patients to distrust their doctors, I believe distrust is more likely to arise from uncertainty about whether a doctor will honor a patient's wishes.[54]

If patients could be sure that fear of the legal consequences would not keep doctors from honoring patients' advance directives or that their own lack of physical strength would not keep them from getting or using the means to commit suicide, supporters like Angell believe, the patients might wait until later in their illness to seek death—or perhaps would not do so at all.

Supporters of assisted suicide deny that it violates traditional medical ethics or trust between doctor and patient. When a doctor cannot heal, they say, his or her job becomes comforting patients and their families and easing their pain. These supporters see causing

An elderly cancer patient is cared for by her daughter at a hospice. Many wonder if such terminally ill individuals should have the right to decide when to die.

the death of incurably ill people at their request as part of the duty to comfort. Ethicist David Orentlicher writes,

If we view physicians fundamentally as relievers of discomfort or disease, with health promotion as part of that role, then assistance with suicide is not only compatible with the physician's role but quite possibly an obligation inherent in it.[55]

Supporters point out that some physicians already blur the distinction between easing pain and causing death. They prescribe high doses of narcotics to control a terminally ill patient's pain, knowing that such doses may also hasten death. Opponents say that this behavior is morally different from assisted suicide because the doctor's purpose is not to kill, even though he or she knows that death may occur.

Death by Misunderstanding

Many people oppose physician-assisted suicide because they fear it will be misused. First, patients may request death inappropriately because they or their doctors misunderstand their condition. This may have happened with Rebecca Badger, for instance. To help prevent suicides based on medical mistakes, many supporters of assisted-suicide laws say that people should have to have a diagnosis, or identification of their medical condition, confirmed by two doctors before their requests for death are granted.

People also sometimes seek death primarily because they suffer from depression. Critics say that many of Jack Kevorkian's patients, including Badger, were probably more depressed than physically ill. A survey of doctors in Washington state revealed that most patients who asked the doctors for help in committing suicide said they did so because they were worried about being dependent or being a burden to their families rather than because they were in pain. This fact supports the idea that mental factors are often more important than physical ones in making patients decide to die. The patients' fears are understandable, but such fears can be a sign of depression.

Depression often can be relieved by drugs and counseling. Even some very ill people have changed their minds about suicide after being given such treatment. Social service advisers, for instance,

can help a family get assistance in caring for someone who is terminally or incurably ill. This can ease the depression of both the sick person and the family members. Counselors can also help people learn to live with severe disability. To keep people who may have treatable depression from committing suicide, some proposed assisted-suicide laws require that a psychiatrist evaluate people who ask for help in dying.

Better Care for the Dying

Opponents of physician-assisted suicide say that people sometimes ask for death when what they really need is better medical care. Almost all pain, these critics say, can be controlled with the right medication. With this and other care, terminally ill patients can be given a peaceful, natural death at home or in a hospice (institution devoted to care of the dying) without hurrying the process. If doctors were better trained in pain management and hospice care, they say, there would be little or no need for assisted suicide. For instance, Edward J. Halloran, a registered nurse, writes,

> Assisted suicide is neither necessary nor desirable when hospice services are initiated [begun]. Maintaining hope, independence, and comfort is a far better choice than suicide or an agonizing death.[56]

Some supporters of hospice care say that such care will never become widely available if assisted suicide is made legal. Arthur Caplan, for example, fears that

> We may end up saying: "We've got assisted suicide—we don't have to worry about fixing up the pathetic nursing home system for the frail, old and disabled. They can kill themselves if they don't like it."[57]

On the other hand, Marcia Angell agrees that more hospice care is needed, but she does not believe that this need conflicts with the need for physician-assisted suicide.

> Good comfort care and the availability of physician-assisted suicide are no more mutually exclusive than good cardiologic [heart] care and the availability of heart transplants.[58]

Supporters of physician-assisted suicide say that, although people who request death should be encouraged to consider alternatives such as hospice care, in the end the patient must be the one who decides whether—and how—his or her life is worth living. Some supporters, though not all, say that this right should extend to people with any illness, not just those who have only a few months to live or are in physical pain.

A Right Becomes a Duty

Much more important than the fear that patients might misuse the right to die is the fear that those around them might abuse it. Through persuasion or even coercion, family members might turn a right to die into a duty to die.

An eighty-four-year-old woman in Santa Rosa, California, who lived with her daughter for twenty years, described how this can happen. She wrote to a local newspaper in 1993:

> When I started to lose my hearing about three years ago, it irritated my daughter. . . . She began to question me about my financial matters and . . . became very rude to me. . . . Then . . . one evening, my daughter said very cautiously she thought it was o.k. for older people to commit suicide if they cannot take care of themselves.

The daughter later repeated this message in various ways, the woman wrote. "So here I sit, day after day," she concluded, "knowing what I am expected to do when I need a little help."[59]

With medical care so likely to be rationed in the future, critics of physician-assisted suicide fear that doctors and managed health care organizations might add their pressure to that of family members. Yale law professor Robert A. Burt, for instance, worries that

> the poor, elderly, unassertive, clinically depressed, members of disfavored minorities or some combination of these— would be especially vulnerable to . . . prompting to choose a quick, easy (and inexpensive) exit.[60]

Similarly, New York attorney general Dennis Vacco, defending his state's law against assisted suicide, warned, "We have the prospect

Reprinted by permission of Chuck Asay and Creators Syndicate.

of managed-care organizations saying it's cheaper to pay for assisted suicide than to pay for treatment or life-sustaining devices."[61]

"Good Death"

Fears of abuse become even greater when people consider progressing beyond assisted suicide to euthanasia, in which a physician causes death directly. The term comes from Greek words meaning "good death." Some supporters of physician-assisted suicide, such as Marcia Angell and David Orentlicher, do not approve of euthanasia because it could be done without a patient's consent. Others see both as equally ethical, provided that euthanasia is done with consent given either at the time or in advance.

To many critics, euthanasia represents the bottom of the slippery slope that society has started down with the legalization of physician-assisted suicide and even, perhaps, the stoppage of lifesaving medical treatment. Some point out that the Nazis in Germany began by supporting euthanasia for severely ill, disabled, or retarded people and ended up trying to engineer the genocide of whole racial groups who, in their opinion, possessed "lives not worth living." If euthanasia is ever legalized in the United States, these people say, something similar might happen. Robert P. George and William C. Porth Jr. write,

> It is not unrealistic to fear that government may assume what began as a private prerogative [right], and move from taking life-and-death decisions for the comatose [people in comas], to making them for the insane, for the retarded, for those of less-than-average intelligence, and finally for those who are entirely rational and intelligent but whose desire to cling to life brands them as . . . uncooperative and . . . unreasonable.[62]

Some supporters of physician-assisted suicide and euthanasia say that the danger of abuse can be eliminated, or at least greatly reduced, by including safeguards in laws that permit these activities. The Oregon assisted-suicide law, for instance, allows a patient's request for a lethal prescription to be granted only after two doctors agree that the patient has a condition that will be fatal within six months or less. The patient must make three requests over a period of at least fifteen days, the last one in writing, and must be certified mentally competent by a doctor.

Members of Not Dead Yet, an organization of disabled people opposed to physician-assisted suicide, protest outside the Supreme Court. Whether physician-assisted suicide should be permitted by law is highly controversial.

Supporters point out that as long as physician-assisted suicide remains illegal, regulations cannot be applied to it because it will be carried out only in secret. Making the activity legal, therefore, could be a first step toward ensuring that it will not be abused. Opponents, however, say that legal safeguards would be hard to enforce.

Experiment in the Netherlands

In trying to foresee what might happen if physician-assisted suicide and euthanasia become legal in the United States, both supporters and opponents have looked to the Netherlands. There, both actions, although illegal, have been openly accepted for over twenty years. Guidelines recommended by the Royal Dutch Medical Association say that euthanasia should be carried out only on mentally competent adults who have voluntarily and consistently requested it over a period of time. They must be suffering with no prospect of relief or cure, but they need not be terminally ill. Doctors are supposed to consult with another doctor before carrying out a patient's request. However, psychiatrist Herbert Hendin points out, "Virtually every guideline established by the Dutch . . . has been modified or violated with impunity [no punishment]."[63]

According to a nationwide study made by the Dutch government in 1990, using anonymous questionnaires distributed to doctors, a little under 3 percent of the deaths in the Netherlands in that year were due to euthanasia or physician-assisted suicide. A second study in 1995 showed similar results. Its authors concluded that "in our view, these data do not support the idea that physicians in the Netherlands are moving down a slippery slope."[64]

Opponents of euthanasia, however, point with alarm to the one thousand deaths (out of about thirty-seven hundred doctor-assisted deaths) that doctors in the 1990 study say they caused in patients who were not mentally competent at the time of death. According to the doctors, over half of these patients had requested euthanasia earlier, when they were competent. Almost all were expected to die within days or weeks. An article in *U.S. News & World Report,* however, claims that 72 percent of these people had not left earlier directives. It says that in 45 percent of the cases the patient's family was not consulted either.

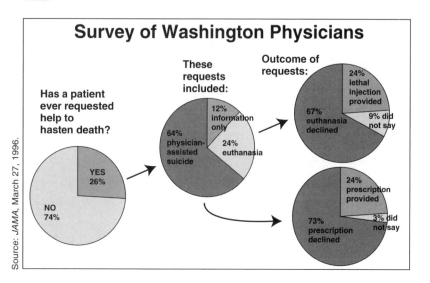

Survey of Washington Physicians

Has a patient ever requested help to hasten death?

NO 74%

YES 26%

These requests included:

64% physician-assisted suicide

12% information only

24% euthanasia

Outcome of requests:

67% euthanasia declined

24% lethal injection provided

9% did not say

73% prescription declined

24% prescription provided

3% did not say

Source: JAMA, March 27, 1996.

Does Legalization Matter?

The results of a 1995 survey of doctors in Washington state suggest that it may not matter much whether physician-assisted suicide and euthanasia are legalized. The situation in Washington, where these actions are against the law, is not very different from that in the Netherlands. The authors of the study write:

> Washington physicians receive requests for physician-assisted suicide or euthanasia almost as frequently as Dutch physicians. . . . Also, physicians in both places grant approximately the same proportion of requests. . . . Patients in both places make these requests regardless of legal constraints on physicians or [differences in] medical care delivery systems. [The Netherlands has a nationalized health care system.][65]

However, say Leon Kass and Nelson Lund,

> That many physicians are already tempted to assist in suicide, and to perform euthanasia, is *not* a reason for changing the traditional rule [against doing so]. On the contrary, it may very well be a warning of how weakened the fragile medical ethic has already become, and how important it is to help shore it up.[66]

In the long run, the frequency of physician-assisted suicide and euthanasia and the extent to which these actions are abused will probably depend more on ethical decisions than on legal ones.

Like the problem of health care rationing, the problem of physician-assisted death has no easy solution. Only open, rational discussion can bring out all sides of the issue. As Stephen L. Carter wrote in *New York Times Magazine,*

> There are strong, thoughtful voices—and plausible moral arguments—on both sides of the assisted-suicide debate, as there are in the larger euthanasia debate. . . . A thoughtful, well-reasoned debate over assisted suicide is . . . what we as a nation need.[67]

Chapter ■3■

Should Animals Be Used in Medical Research and Testing?

B EFORE SUNUP ON JULY 4, 1989, members of an organization called the Animal Liberation Front (ALF) broke into a laboratory in Lubbock, Texas, belonging to John Orem of Texas Tech University. They smashed several expensive lab instruments and stole five cats that were being used in Orem's research on breathing disorders during sleep. Such disorders include Sudden Infant Death Syndrome, or "crib death," which mysteriously kills about five thousand babies during their sleep every year.

The raid was only part of the attack on Orem. People for the Ethical Treatment of Animals (PETA), a large animal rights organization that often publicizes the work of smaller groups like ALF, issued press releases saying that Orem "abuses, mutilates, and kills animals" and calling him and other biomedical researchers "animal-Nazis."[68]

A month after the raid, PETA filed a formal complaint with the National Institutes of Health (NIH), the federal research organization that provided funds for Orem's work and that of many other researchers who use animals in their research. PETA cited sixteen people, whom they claimed were experts, who said that Orem's work was "cruel"[69] and lacked scientific significance. None of these people, however, had ever been in Orem's laboratory or had any experience in his area of research.

The NIH chose a group of scientists who were experienced in neuroscience, veterinary medicine, and other fields related to Orem's work. The scientists inspected Orem's laboratory on September 18.

They reported back that ALF's claims were unfounded and that his work was "important and of the highest scientific quality."[70]

Animal Sacrifices

Who was right—PETA's experts or those from NIH? And even if the scientists from NIH were right, did the value of John Orem's work really give him the right to experiment on the animals in his laboratory? Orem's research is part of a long tradition of sacrificing animals' comfort, health, and even lives to advance medical science. When, if ever, is such sacrifice ethical?

Many supporters of what has come to be called the animal rights movement would say seldom or never. They believe that use of animals in medical research and testing violates the animals' right to live a free life and not be subjected to unnatural stress or pain. Most medical researchers, on the other hand, say that the use of animals in research and testing is ethical because it improves human health. They believe that the benefits of such research to humans far outweigh any harm that the animals suffer.

AIDS activists and animal rights activists clash during a demonstration in Washington, D.C., in 1996. Many animal rights activists are opposed to all experimentation on animals.

Partly because of animal rights groups' protests and their push for alternatives to the use of animals, the number of animals used in biomedical research has dropped sharply in recent years. In 1986 the U.S. Office of Technology Assessment estimated that 17 to 22 million vertebrate animals (animals with backbones, including mammals, birds, and fish) were used in laboratory experiments or testing in the United States each year. Since then, according to several estimates, the number has fallen by 30 percent or more.

Still, the number of mice and rats (which make up about 85 percent of all laboratory animals) used in research remains in the millions. Hundreds of thousands of rabbits, guinea pigs, hamsters, cattle, sheep, and dogs, and lesser numbers of cats and primates (apes and monkeys) are still used, and sometimes killed, in U.S. laboratories each year. Animals obviously still play a major part in research and testing, and the ethics of their use is an important medical issue.

Are Humans More Valuable than Animals?

Some people who oppose animal use in research believe that animals are just as morally valuable as humans. They say that any research that cannot ethically be performed on humans is also unethical if performed on animals. Donald Barnes of the National Anti-Vivisection Society writes,

> I consider the inducement of stress, pain and suffering to nonhuman animals for the . . . sake of human beings . . . to be immoral. . . . *There are no morally relevant differences between humans and nonhumans.*[71]

Or, as Ingrid Newkirk, cofounder of PETA has bluntly put it, "A rat is a pig is a dog is a boy."[72]

At the other extreme, some people think that humans have a far greater value than animals. They claim that key differences such as consciousness, the ability to use language, or the power to make moral judgments and contracts set humans apart from other living things.

Australian philosopher Peter Singer, one of the founders of the modern animal rights movement, calls valuing one's own species above all others "speciesism." In his 1975 book, *Animal Liberation,* Singer said that speciesism is as morally unjustified as racism or

Animal rights demonstrators protest outside a meeting of the American Psychological Association. Animals are used in psychological research.

sexism. On the other hand, physician and ethicist Carl Cohen writes that "speciesism . . . is essential for right conduct."[73] Cohen says that only humans have rights because only humans can make moral judgments. In a 1988 article in *Newsweek,* Jane McCabe defended her speciesism in a more personal way:

> My daughter has cystic fibrosis [a disease, caused by a genetic defect, that harms the lungs]. Her only hope for a normal life is that researchers, some of them using animals, will find a cure. . . . It's not that I don't love animals, it's just that I love Claire more.[74]

Many ethicists take a position between these two extremes. They give humans a higher value than animals, but they say that animals have moral value. For instance, Jean Bethke Elshtain wrote in the *Progressive,*

> I . . . do not believe humans and animals have identical rights. But I do believe that creatures who can reason in their own ways, who can suffer, . . . have a value and dignity we must take into account. Animals are not simply a means to our ends.[75]

Benefits of Research

Medical researchers who experiment on animals usually consider their work ethical because of the benefits it brings to humans. In a 1990 *Reader's Digest* article, for instance, John G. Hubbell wrote,

> Animal research has led to vaccines against diphtheria, polio, measles, mumps, whooping cough, rubella [German measles]. It has meant eradication [elimination] of smallpox, effective treatment for diabetes and control of infection with powerful antibiotics. The cardiac [heart] pacemaker, microsurgery to reattach severed limbs, and heart, kidney, lung, liver and other transplants are all possible because of animal research.[76]

Future successes in research, supporters say, will depend equally heavily on the use of animals. "Without animal research, medical science would come to a total standstill,"[77] best-selling author and physician Lewis Thomas has written.

Animal rights activists, however, dispute the idea that human health and life expectancy have improved in the twentieth century chiefly because of research on animals. According to emergency room physician and animal rights supporter Peggy Carlson, researchers at Harvard and Boston Universities found that only between 1 and 3.5 percent of the total decline in the death rate in the United States since 1900 is due to medical treatments such as drugs and vaccines. The university study claimed that most of the decline resulted from a drop in deaths from microbe-caused diseases such as tuberculosis and smallpox, which was already occurring before antibiotics and other treatments for the diseases were developed. The reduction in deaths was probably caused by improved sanitation and diet.

Similar or Different?

Animals are used in medical research and testing because scientists believe that they are similar to humans in key biological ways. For instance, Richard McCourt wrote in *Discover* magazine,

> Any little mammal will provide a reasonable analogy to a human. . . . Our hemoglobins [oxygen-carrying substance in blood], cell membranes, and many enzymes [important cell

chemicals] are so similar that what's true for one is often true for the other.[78]

Opponents of animal research, on the other hand, stress the differences between animals and humans. They say these differences are so great that the results of research or testing on animals cannot truly be applied to people. "I am convinced that the use of nonhuman animals as surrogates [substitutes] for other animals, humans or nonhuman, constitutes poor science,"[79] says Donald Barnes.

Humans are unquestionably both like and unlike other animals. Ethically, this mixture of similarities and differences creates what Peter Singer has called "the researcher's central dilemma":

A group of animal rights activists protest at a primate research center operated by Harvard University. Many activists protest the experimental use of higher-level animals such as primates, which are close to humans in their complexity of thought.

Either the animal is not like us, in which case there is no
reason for performing the experiment; or else the animal is
like us, in which case we ought not to perform an experiment on the animal which would be considered wrong if
performed on one of us.[80]

Where to Draw the Line

Some members of the animal rights movement say that no use of
animals for medical research—or for any other purpose that benefits
humans at animals' expense—is justified. "It's not better cages we
work for, but empty cages," says animal rights leader Tom Regan.
"We want every animal out."[81]

Some people who see no moral difference between humans and
animals do not take such an extreme position, however. For
instance, Bernard E. Rollin, director of bioethical planning at Colorado State University, noted that a belief in moral equality between
humans and animals would not eliminate all research on animals
because some research on humans is considered ethical.

Many ethicists—and most members of the public—find some biomedical uses of animals ethical but not others. As with health care
rationing and physician-assisted death, they differ in where they draw
the line on the slippery slope between ethical and unethical conduct.

In judging individual experiments, most people follow a utilitarian approach, weighing the possible benefits of the research
against the harm it does. They consider the purpose of the research,
its effectiveness, the amount of suffering it causes to animals, and
the types of animals involved. The basic utilitarian standard for
judging research on animals, says Bernard Rollin, is "that the benefit to humans (or to humans and animals) clearly outweighs the pain
and suffering experienced by the experimental animals."[82]

Saving Human Lives

The type of research most likely to be considered ethical is that which
seeks ways to prevent, treat, or cure serious human diseases or tries to
make basic discoveries about the way human bodies work. Animals can
be used as substitutes or "models" for humans in both kinds of research.

One deadly human disease now being studied partly through animal research is AIDS. AIDS activists differ in their feelings about this form of research. Not surprisingly, perhaps, Jeff Getty, who has received animal bone marrow as a treatment for AIDS, urges more research on animals. He and nine other AIDS patients blocked traffic outside an animal rights demonstration in Washington, D.C., in December 1995, carrying signs saying "Rights for lab rats over my dead body."[83] On the other hand, Steven I. Simmons, who is both an AIDS activist and a member of PETA, claims that animal research on AIDS should be stopped because it is useless. He disagrees with researchers who claim that chimpanzees develop AIDS when injected with the virus that causes the human disease: "AIDS is a uniquely human phenomenon."[84]

A second purpose for using animals in medicine is to provide substances that help to identify, treat, or prevent human illnesses. For many years, for instance, animals have been a source of certain hormones, important body chemicals that send messages between cells. Insulin, necessary to preserve the lives of people with diabetes, came from cattle until recently. Estrogen, a hormone that

AIDS activist and baboon bone marrow recipient Jeff Getty (left) takes part in a protest outside a meeting of the World Congress for Animals. A beneficiary of animal research, Getty opposes its discontinuance.

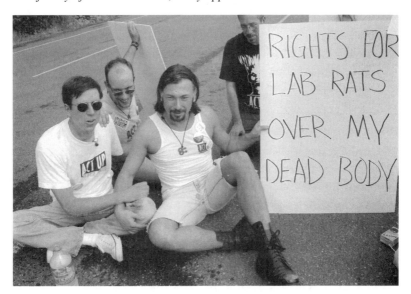

many older women take to prevent weakening of bones and other problems, is often extracted from the urine of pregnant mares (female horses). Some vaccines, which prevent microbe-caused diseases by increasing immunity, must also be produced in animals.

Most people seem to feel that using animals as sources for medical products is ethical unless the extraction process causes great pain or death that would not otherwise occur. (In many cases, the products come from animals that are being slaughtered anyway for meat.) Some animal rights groups, however, object to using animals as medical "factories," just as they object to using animals to make meat, leather, or other products for human consumption.

New Uses for Animals

The use of animals as sources for medical products is expanding in new ways today because of advances in genetic engineering. Human genes (units of hereditary information) that contain instructions for making certain hormones can be placed in the cells of cattle and sheep, for instance. The animals then produce hormones identical to human ones. Carol Grunewald of the Humane Society of the United States says, "Genetic engineering represents the most extreme and blatant form of animal exploitation yet."[85] However, Caroline Murphy, education officer for the Royal Society for Prevention of Cruelty to Animals in England, writes,

> We must neither assume that all genetic engineering [of animals] is evil, nor be seduced into thinking that the bright light of science can offer only progress. . . . We must ensure that we regulate . . . this new technique to the benefit of both ourselves and other animals.[86]

In the future, advances in genetic engineering may let animals be used as sources for a new kind of medical product: hearts or other organs to be transplanted into humans. This could ease the organ shortage that must now be handled by rationing. "Scarcity . . . grounds the moral case for thinking about animals as sources of organs and tissues,"[87] writes Arthur Caplan.

Some animal rights leaders and bioethicists, however, question whether scarcity is a good enough reason for killing animals. For

Dr. Karl Ebert is surrounded by some of the first genetically manipulated goats capable of producing large quantities of human proteins in their milk. One of the goats produced up to five ounces a day of a protein used to treat a form of emphysema. Use of animals as living biological factories is highly controversial.

example, bioethicist James Lindemann Nelson of the Hastings Center in New York writes,

> We're at a loss to say what it is about baboons that makes their livers fair game, when we wouldn't dare take vital organs from those of our own species whose abilities to live rich, full lives are no greater than those of the nonhumans we seem so willing to prey upon. Unless we're able to isolate and defend the relevant moral distinction, we should reject the seductive image of solving the problem of organ shortage by maintaining colonies of animals . . . for transplantation.[88]

Drug Testing

A third common purpose for using animals in research is the testing of drugs and other medical treatments. Indeed, more animals are used in testing than in pure research.

Almost all new drugs and treatments are tested on animals before being tried on humans. Most countries, including the United States and

Britain, require such testing before the products can be sold. Nonetheless, some people question whether using animals to test medical treatments is medically or morally justifiable. "Animal testing is one of the most wasteful and incredibly cumbersome methodologies in science today,"[89] says Neal Barnard, president of the Physicians Committee for Responsible Medicine. On the other hand, many researchers feel that animal testing is necessary for safety. Ernst Knobil, former president of the American Physiological Society, says:

> In the testing of polio vaccine, where a small error could paralyze hundreds of children, I would not want to have my child or grandchild inoculated with a product that had not been submitted to the most rigorous [careful] testing procedures, which include administration of the vaccine to . . . monkeys and the careful examination of their brains and spinal cords afterwards.[90]

Many people oppose some tests but not others. Some tests, they say, save human lives by eliminating useless or dangerous drugs. Others, however, cause great suffering and death to animals and at

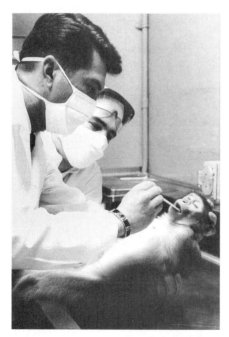

A monkey used to test polio vaccine is examined by doctors to verify its health. Many physicians believe that the sacrifice of animals, including monkeys, is justified when it means saving human lives.

the same time are too crude or poorly designed to tell researchers anything useful.

The test that has been most widely criticized for these reasons is called the LD50 (Lethal Dose 50). It determines the dose of a substance that causes death in 50 percent of a group of animals within fourteen days. Usually between forty and two hundred mammals, most often mice or rats, are tested at a time. This test is applied not only to drugs but to substances that normally would never be swallowed, such as cosmetics and household products.

The LD50 test has been a standard part of early drug and product testing since it was introduced in 1927. Many companies still use it, and some regulatory agencies demand it. However, Bernard Rollin, for one, jokingly claims that this test is useful only to "tell mice what dose of a chemical they need in order to commit suicide effectively."[91] He points out that it shows nothing about the risks of small, repeated doses of a substance taken over long periods—the way medication is usually taken. It also shows nothing about what happens to the substance in the body. For these reasons, says Rollin, the LD50 test is virtually useless in predicting how poisonous a substance will be to humans. It also causes great suffering even to the animals that survive it. Many animal rights groups, and quite a few researchers, would like to see it banned.

Suffering Monkeys

In addition to judging experiments or tests on animals according to their purpose and effectiveness, people evaluate research according to the amount of suffering it causes for animals. Even when tests or experiments are potentially helpful to humans, people may find them unethical if they cause great pain to animals or if the animals are poorly cared for during the research.

The U.S. Department of Agriculture (USDA) reported in 1994 that of animals covered under the Animal Welfare Act (which includes most mammals but does not include mice and rats), 54 percent experienced no pain or distress during experiments. Thirty-five percent suffered pain or distress that was relieved by drugs. Only 11 percent suffered pain and distress that was not relieved because painkilling drugs would interfere with the research results. However, notes Martin Stephens of the Humane Society of the United States, the number of animals actually suffering may be higher:

> The categories [used by the USDA] are poorly defined . . . [and] do not account for any suffering that stems from barren and cramped housing conditions, rough handling, outright abuse, and other non-experimental causes.[92]

Accusations of mistreatment during research were the focus of a 1981 case that helped bring the animal rights movement to public attention in the United States. The alleged mistreatment occurred in the laboratory of Edward Taub at the Institute for Behavioral Research in Silver Spring, Maryland. Taub was trying to find ways to help people paralyzed by strokes or injuries to the spinal cord. To mimic these conditions, he cut the nerves in the arms of eight monkeys.

Bored in their tiny cages, the monkeys began chewing at themselves. Pain did not stop them because the cut nerves kept them from feeling pain. The monkeys received no veterinary care and lived in

---

Members of People for the Ethical Treatment of Animals dress as monkeys in prison suits and block the entrance to the Department of Health and Human Services. PETA opposes the use of animals in research, believing that humans do not have a right to inflict pain on animals.

quarters that were seldom cleaned. As a result, their wounds soon became festering sores.

A twenty-three-year-old college student named Alex Pacheco worked in Taub's laboratory. Pacheco was already deeply concerned about animal abuse; he and Ingrid Newkirk had founded PETA the year before. Shocked at the monkeys' condition, he secretly began taking photographs of them. One night he let several experts into the lab to see the animals for themselves. He took his photos and the experts' reports to the Maryland police and demanded that the laboratory be raided.

The police raided Taub's laboratory on September 11, 1981, and charged him with seventeen counts of cruelty to animals. All the charges were eventually dropped. Still, the case made national headlines, and the public looked with horror at the pictures Pacheco had taken. The NIH, the federal government agency that funds much of the medical research done in the United States, canceled the large grant that supported Taub's research.

Guidelines for Animal Care

Researchers insist that mistreatment of lab animals is uncommon today. For instance, veterinary technician Jessica Szymczyk, writing in *Newsweek* in 1995, says that she is a vegetarian and "absolutely love[s] animals," yet she also loves her work in a drug company laboratory that uses animals. She claims that 95 percent of the procedures in her laboratory "are less painful [to the animals] than a visit to the doctor for you and me." She describes the laboratory itself as "clean, well lit and modern . . . like a human hospital"[93] and pictures its "frisky, playful" dogs enjoying frequent contact with animal technicians like herself.

To prevent abuse, most American and Western European countries have created guidelines for the care of laboratory animals. One such set of guidelines, the Animal Welfare Act (AWA), was drawn up in 1966. All U.S. laboratories that receive federal funding must abide by it. It covers primates, dogs, cats, rabbits, guinea pigs, and hamsters. The AWA and related guidelines have been revised several times, most recently in 1996. They not only specify such things as cage size but instruct researchers to provide "environmental enrichment" for the animals and to increase their "psychological well-being." The guidelines also require local committees to review proposals for research using animals. These committees include scientists, veterinarians, and members of the public.

Animal rights advocates have criticized the AWA for several reasons. First, they point out, it does not cover mice and rats, by far the most common laboratory animals. They also say it is vague (how does someone measure "environmental enrichment" or "psychological well-being"?) and inadequately enforced. As for the review committees, Martin Stephens says,

> [The committee] members from outside the institution who are supposed to represent community concerns . . . typically are not known by (nor do they communicate with) animal protection advocates. Few . . . [committee] meetings are open to the public, and their effectiveness in screening inappropriate, redundant, and/or inhumane experiments is questionable.[94]

A physician holds a cat used in experiments in a laboratory at the University of California at Berkeley. Many researchers contend that the animals used in their work are well treated and suffer little or no pain.

Overall, Stephens claims, "The AWA . . . has little effect on actual experimental procedures."[95]

Which Kind of Animal?

Another standard on which many people judge the ethics of particular uses of animals in research is the kind of animal involved. Most animal rights groups do not oppose the use of, say, bacteria or insects in research. These animals' simple nervous systems do not let them feel pain in the way mammals do. Among mammals, most people feel little concern about mice and rats, which they see as pests. On the other hand, they are likely to object to experiments on cats and dogs because many people love these kinds of animals as pets.

The strongest ethical objections are reserved for nonhuman primates because these animals are so similar to people. Chimpanzees share 98.6 percent of humans' genetic information. This close resemblance to human beings makes these animals especially valuable in some kinds of medical experiments. However, that same resemblance means that apes suffer mental distress when confined in laboratories, much as people would. Furthermore, chimpanzees and some other primates are endangered in the wild. Capturing them for medical research reduces their numbers still further.

To some ethicists, experimenting on a chimpanzee is much like experimenting on a developmentally disabled child. They say that research using apes should either be banned entirely or be permitted only when it is likely to benefit humanity greatly. If such animals are used, they should be kept with others of their kind in a stimulating environment.

Arthur Caplan, however, defends the ethics of using nonhuman primates rather than human beings in research:

> The case for using animals, even primates, before using a human being with severely limited abilities and capacities [for research] is based on the relationships that exist among human beings, which do not have parallels in the animal kingdom. These relationships, such as love, loyalty, . . . sympathy, family-feeling, protectiveness, . . . community-mindedness, . . . and a sense of responsibility, . . . ground many moral duties.[96]

Replace, Reduce, Refine

Whatever their exact position on the use of animals in medical research, most scientists, members of the public, and animal rights supporters agree that the number of animals used in research should be cut down as much as possible. British researchers William M. S. Russell and Rex L. Burch have called the paths to this goal the "three R's": Replace, Reduce, and Refine.

Increasingly, mammals can be replaced in experiments and tests by other tools, including computer simulations, cells or tissues grown in the laboratory, and simpler animals. Most scientists are glad to use alternative tests because they are usually faster and cheaper—and sometimes more accurate—than tests on animals. "From an animal activist's perspective, the past decade has been very encouraging in promoting alternatives to traditional animal testing,"[97] animal rights leader Henry Spira reported in 1994.

The number of good alternatives to animal testing is likely to increase. Alternatives may never replace all research on animals, however. "You cannot study kidney transplantation or diarrhea or high blood pressure on a computer screen,"[98] maintains Bessie Borwein of the University of Western Ontario in Canada.

A biologist holds a milk bottle in which normal and mutant fruit flies are raised. These flies are used in genetic research because they multiply very rapidly. Many animal rights activists do not oppose the use of insects in animal research because insects cannot feel pain in the way that humans and higher animals do.

Even when tests or experiments on animals could be replaced by alternatives, such replacement does not always occur. Perhaps the most important reason is that regulatory agencies such as the U.S. Food and Drug Administration, which must approve all drugs and medical treatments sold in the country, often have not yet accepted alternative tests as replacements for the traditional animal ones. Other obstacles, according to Jean Bethke Elshtain, are "old habits, bad science, unreflective cruelty, and profit."[99]

Even when animals cannot be replaced entirely, their number can be reduced. The LD50 test, for instance, has been redesigned to use only six to ten animals per test instead of forty to two hundred. In addition, tests and experiments can be refined so that more useful information is obtained from each one.

How Should Animals Be Protected?

People who want to reduce the number of animals in biomedical research and protect their welfare disagree about the best way to do so. A few animal rights groups, such as the Animal Liberation Front, think this aim can best be accomplished by surprise raids on laboratories that they consider abusive. In such raids, protesters often smash expensive scientific equipment, destroy research notes, and "liberate" laboratory animals. Supporters of this tactic say that the raids frighten scientists into treating animals better. They also make headlines that alert the public to laboratory animals' plight.

Most animal rights groups disavow such violent behavior, however. They realize that it harms their own image at least as much as that of the scientists they raid. "When property or life is threatened or harmed," says chimpanzee expert Jane Goodall, "then I think . . . it's counterproductive."[100] Most animal rights groups work peacefully for their aims through techniques such as public education and letter-writing campaigns that put pressure on legislators.

Even when physical violence is not used, both supporters and critics of animal rights often resort to violent language. Bernard Rollin is one of many who think that the situation of animals in biomedical research is most likely to improve if researchers and animal rights supporters learn to have dialogues rather than shouting matches. He writes,

*Researchers survey the damage
done to the University of
Pennsylvania's animal
research lab after an Animal
Liberation Front raid of the
facility. Most animal rights
groups do not use such
destructive tactics.*

The traditional rhetoric [language] that has characterized
the debate between proponents [supporters] and opponents
of research [on animals] . . . has served as an insurmount-
able barrier to . . . the determination of common ground. In
addition to the invective . . . hurled by both sides ("Sadis-
tic vivisectionist"; "Bleeding heart humaniac"; "You would
stop us from curing leukemia"; "You torture kittens for
fun," etc.), the situation has been characterized by abysmal
ignorance on both sides.[101]

Animals can be most effectively protected, he concludes, by those
who are willing to listen to their fellow human beings.

Chapter 4

Should Human Genes Be Altered?

U NTIL THE LATE 1980s, parents had little choice about how tall their children would grow to be. That was determined mostly by the children's genes, the coded information in every cell of their bodies that they inherited from their parents. Many parents believed that being tall gave children, especially boys, an advantage in life, but it was not an advantage they could choose to supply.

The only children whose height could be changed by medication were those few who had a rare condition called pituitary dwarfism. A child with this condition is abnormally short because the child's pituitary, a tiny gland buried deep in the brain, fails to make growth hormone. Human growth hormone (HGH) could be extracted only from the pituitary glands of dead bodies, so treatment with it was difficult and expensive. There was no question of applying this treatment to anyone other than pituitary dwarfs.

In the late 1980s, however, a company called Genentech began to market HGH that it had made artificially through the new technology of genetic engineering. It placed the human gene that contained the information for making growth hormone into bacteria, which then began to produce the compound in large amounts. As a result, supplies of HGH became far greater than the small quantity needed to treat pituitary dwarfs.

Pressured by parents who had heard about the hormone and, perhaps, by Genentech's advertisements, some doctors began to give HGH to children who were simply shorter than average—a condition that had never previously been considered a disease. The hormone treatment seldom helped these children, because they did

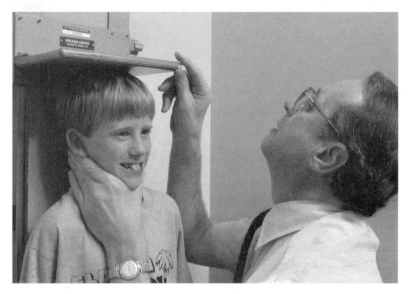

A doctor measures the height of a boy who has been taking human growth hormone. Growth hormone is controversial as a treatment for children who are merely shorter than average.

not lack growth hormone. It sometimes also had serious unwanted results, or side effects.

In the future, it may become possible to directly alter the genes that determine height. When this happens, some people fear, that power may be misused in the same way that HGH was. They say that few, if any, changes in human genes should be permitted. Others say that changing genes offers miraculous new hope of curing disease and perhaps even improving the human species. Where should the line be drawn on the slippery slope presented by this exciting but frightening new technology?

A New World for Ashanthi

Gene therapy, or treating disease by changing genes, first became a reality for humans on September 14, 1990. The first person to benefit from gene therapy was a four-year-old girl named Ashanthi deSilva.

Ashanthi had been sick for most of her life. She had one infection after another, often becoming so ill that she had to stay in a hospital. The body's immune system fights off most illnesses in normal children, but Ashanthi's immune system was helpless to resist germs that attacked her. She had been born without a certain gene, just one of the over one-hundred-thousand bits of information coded into the structure of a complex chemical called DNA. This gene contained instructions for making a key chemical that her immune system needed. Because of this missing gene, Ashanthi seemed doomed to a short and unhappy life.

On that September day, as Ashanthi watched *Sesame Street* from her hospital bed, a river of immune system cells flowed into her bloodstream through a tube in her arm. They were her own cells, taken from her blood two weeks earlier. The cells had spent those weeks in a laboratory, where a team of doctors from the National Institutes of Health (NIH) had used genetic engineering to insert into some of them the gene Ashanthi lacked.

Genetic engineering began in the early 1970s, when scientists learned how to move genes from one living thing to another. Human beings were first given cells with changed genes in 1989, but those genes acted only as markers; they had no effect on the health of the cancer patients who received them. Ashanthi deSilva was the first

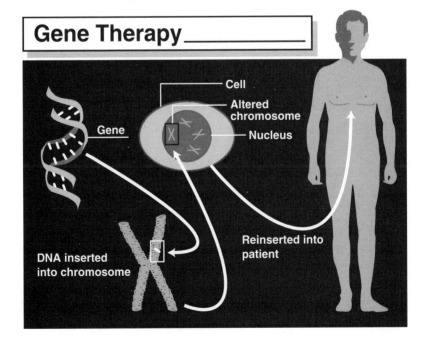

Gene Therapy

person to be given genetically engineered cells as a medical treatment.

Ashanthi's gene therapy was successful. Five years after it took place, W. French Anderson, one of the leaders of the team who treated her, described her as "a healthy, vibrant nine-year-old who loves life and does *everything*."[102] Scientists have gone on to try gene therapy against some thirty other diseases, ranging from rare conditions like Ashanthi's to cancer and AIDS. Sometimes the treatments have worked, sometimes not. As of late 1996, about fifteen hundred human beings worldwide had received some form of altered genes.

A Dangerous Beginning?

Most people have felt that when gene therapy is used on seriously ill people like Ashanthi, it raises no more ethical questions than any other experimental medical treatment. According to Anderson,

> Somatic cell gene therapy [therapy that affects only the body cells of an individual] for the treatment of severe disease is . . . ethical because it can be supported by the fundamental moral principle of beneficence: It would relieve human suffering. Gene therapy would, therefore, be a moral good [under those circumstances].[103]

Yet some critics see even this seemingly helpful treatment as the top of a slippery slope that could lead to genocide of disabled people or even a complete redefinition of being human. For this reason, they oppose any alteration of human genes. Jeremy Rifkin, head of the Foundation on Economic Trends and one of the severest critics of genetic engineering, wrote in his 1983 book, *Algeny:*

> Once we decide to begin the process of human genetic engineering, there really is no logical place to stop. If diabetes, sickle-cell disease [a severe, inherited blood disease], and cancer are to be cured by altering the genetic makeup of an individual, why not proceed to other "disorders": myopia [nearsightedness], color blindness, left handedness. Indeed, what is to preclude [stop] a society from deciding that a certain skin color is a disorder?[104]

(Above) Doctors discuss a new genetic therapy treatment at the National Institutes of Health. The treatment splices new genes into diseased cells and was used successfully on four-year-old Ashanthi deSilva. (Left) Jeremy Rifkin wants to set strict controls on such research, believing that doctors will not place such controls on themselves.

On the other hand, Ola Mae Huntley, a mother of three children with sickle-cell disease, says,

> I am very angry that anyone would presume to deny children and my family the essential genetic treatment for genetic disease. . . . I see such persons as simplistic moralists who probably have seen too many mad scientist horror films.[105]

Because of fears like Rifkin's, many ethicists have agreed that, as biology professors Clifford Grobstein and Michael Flower say, "only a disease that drastically reduces the quality or duration of life should be a candidate for . . . gene therapy."[106] Most of the five hundred Americans surveyed in a *Time* magazine/CNN poll in 1993 felt the same way.

What Is a Defect?

Today, when gene therapy is difficult, expensive, and somewhat risky, limiting it to serious diseases is easy. In ten or twenty years, however, gene treatments will probably be as common as organ transplants are today. As Jeremy Rifkin and some others fear, gene therapy might then be applied, perhaps forcibly, to people who have any trait that is seen as a defect. Evan Kemp, a disabled man who at the time was commissioner of the Equal Employment Opportunity Commission, told a committee considering possible gene therapy experiments in 1989:

> Our society seems to have an aversion to [dislike of] those who are physically and mentally different. Genetic engineering could lead to the elimination of the rich diversity in our peoples. It is a real and frightening threat.[107]

Perhaps worse still, as geneticist Karl A. Drlica wrote in 1994, "What we now call an average child may eventually be considered defective."[108] For instance, children who are healthy but shorter than average might have their genes altered to make them taller, just as some short children were given human growth hormone in the past.

Potential misuses of gene therapy might not be confined to physical traits. Although scientists disagree about how much heredity influences such characteristics as intelligence, aggression, and sexual preference, there is some evidence that genes do help to determine these things. If single genes that increase the tendency to show certain mental characteristics or behaviors are identified, parents—or governments—might be tempted to use gene therapy to remove mental traits that they object to or add ones that they consider desirable.

Not everyone thinks that altering human genes would necessarily be bad, however, even if it were done for trivial reasons. The editor of the *Economist,* a British magazine, wrote in 1992:

Should people be able to retrofit themselves with [genes] . . . to enhance various mental powers? Or to change the colour of their skin? Or to help them run faster, or lift heavier weights? Yes, they should. . . . People have a right to make what they want of their lives . . . [unless the] alterations [are] clearly likely to cause harm to others.[109]

Pressure to Change Genes

Critics such as Paul Billings, deputy chief of staff at the Veterans Affairs Medical Center in Palo Alto, California, worry that if gene therapy becomes easily available, people might be pressured to use it on themselves or their children. In an attempt to cut the costs of care they would have to pay for, health insurance companies or managed care organizations might refuse to accept people who do not alter genes that cause or increase the risk of disease. Employers, who often provide health insurance to their employees, might refuse to hire such people. Prospective mates might not want to have children with those whose genes they see as defective. As a result, people who do not wish to—or cannot afford to—"correct" their genes might become a new underclass.

Prenatal testing can now identify the genes for dozens of inherited diseases in unborn children. Pressure has already been put on

'I'm sorry we can't choose the baby's gender, but for a private patient I can genetically alter its colouring to match your decor.'

some parents whose unborn babies carry such genes to use the only "gene therapy" presently available for most: abortion. For instance, a California woman who belonged to a managed health care organization learned that she was carrying a child that would be born with cystic fibrosis, a serious hereditary disorder. The organization offered to pay for an abortion, but it refused to pay for the child's care if the woman insisted on giving birth to it. Only the threat of a lawsuit forced the company to change its mind.

Discrimination has also affected people who themselves carry "bad genes," even though they are not ill. For example, the U.S. Air Force turned down two recruits because they were carriers of the gene that causes sickle-cell disease, even though the men would never develop the disease. For many inherited diseases, including sickle-cell disease, a person must inherit two copies of the defective gene, one from the mother and one from the father, in order to show the disease. People who inherit one defective and one normal copy of the gene are called carriers. They can pass the defective gene on to their children, but they themselves will never suffer from the disease.

Paul Billings published a study in January 1996 that cited 455 cases of people being denied insurance, health care, jobs, schooling, or the right to adopt children because of a family history of hereditary disease. Billings fears that, in the future, "every risk assessment event could be linked to gene tests: your driver's license, gun permit, home mortgage."[110] However, some supporters of gene therapy feel that growing availability of such therapy will remove the threat of genetic discrimination rather than make it worse. For instance, British geneticist Walter Bodmer claims that

> the current predicaments of genetic screening should disappear once technology can put right the mutated culprits that it uncovers. . . . Abortions [for genetic defects] will no longer be necessary because we will be able to correct those life-threatening faulty genes.[111]

Changing Future Generations

So far, the only genes that have been changed in human beings have been those in somatic, or body, cells. These cells live, at most, as long as the person of whom they are a part. Most live a much shorter time. Ashanthi deSilva, for instance, has had to have multiple gene treatments because the engineered blood cells she receives eventually grow old and die. If a person undergoes somatic-cell gene therapy and later has children, the changes in the person's genes will not be passed on to those children.

In the future, however, it will almost surely be possible to change the genes of human germ-line cells—the sperm and eggs that pass genetic information on to the next generation. Genetic engineers can already produce germ-line changes in mice and some other animals. The possibility of altering germ-line genes raises ethical questions even more serious than those raised by changing body-cell genes because germ-line changes become a permanent part of inheritance.

Some scientists feel that removing genes that cause serious or life-threatening diseases from a family's germ line would be ethical. Why, they say, should each generation have to undergo the expense and risks of somatic-cell gene therapy when the problem could be solved once and for all? Walter Bodmer says, "Removing an obvious,

Two years after her ground-breaking gene therapy, Ashanthi deSilva mixes colored sand in elementary school. Whether gene therapy should be used remains controversial despite such lifesaving successes.

fatal mutant [abnormal gene] from the human gene pool would . . . be unequivocally [unquestionably] beneficial for mankind."[112]

Clifford Grobstein and Michael Flower even believe that *not* removing defective genes from the human germ line might be unethical.

> If reproductive health includes the probability of having genetically normal offspring, . . . [an] individual [with a disease caused by defective genes] could claim an ethical right not to be deprived of germ-line repair since, without it, all offspring would at least be carriers [of the defective gene]. . . . The argument to rid the lineage [line of descendants] of the defective genes once and for all might prove compelling.[113]

Others feel that changes in the genes of germ-line cells should never be allowed. A resolution signed and presented to Congress in 1983 by fifty-six religious leaders as well as eight scientists and ethicists stated that "efforts to engineer specific genetic traits into the germ line of the human species should not be attempted."[114] Similarly, Canadian geneticist David Suzuki states as a basic "genethic principle":

> While genetic manipulation of human somatic cells may lie in the realm of personal choice, tinkering with human germ cells does not. Germ-cell therapy, without the consent of all members of society, ought to be explicitly forbidden.[115]

Why Not Change Germ-Line Genes?

One objection to changing germ-line cells is that doing so violates the rights of the unborn by performing actions on them without their consent. The same *Economist* editorial that supported the right of people to change their own genes in any way they wished went on to say,

> No one should have his genes changed without his informed consent; to force genetic change on another without his consent is a violation of his person, a crime as severe as rape or grievous bodily harm.[116]

Other critics of germ-line therapy question whether scientists will ever have enough knowledge to judge whether a gene is truly

"defective." For instance, the gene that causes sickle-cell disease in people who inherit two copies of it is common among people of African descent. The disease is painful and disabling, so this gene might seem a good candidate for removal from the germ line. However, researchers have learned that people who carry just one copy of the sickle-cell gene are resistant to malaria. Malaria, a serious blood disease, is caused by a microscopic parasite that is common in many parts of Africa. Thus the sickle-cell gene may have given Africans who carried one copy of it better health than those who lacked it.

Other disease-causing genes may have similar hidden benefits. By removing germ-line genes that cause disease under some conditions, scientists might unknowingly deprive humans of characteristics that could be helpful in other conditions. "Are we wise enough to ignore millions of years of evolution, which has brought us . . . these . . . traits?"[117] Jeremy Rifkin asks.

Creating a "Master Race"

Germ-line gene therapy critics' greatest fear—the bottom of the slippery slope—is that a government or an elite class might use such therapy to permanently alter human genes in ways that have nothing to do with health. They could add characteristics that they find desirable and remove those of which they disapprove. In doing so, they might redefine what it means to be human. Canadian biologist N. J. Berill has predicted:

> Sooner or later one human society or another will launch out on this adventure [of using gene alteration to produce people with certain characteristics], whether the rest of mankind approves or not. If this happens, and a superior race emerges with greater intelligence and longer lives, how will these people look upon those who are lagging behind? . . . They, not we, will be the heirs to the future, and they will assume control.[118]

People who oppose germ-line alteration because of fears that someone will try to use it to create a "master race" point to actions taken earlier in this century by followers of a now-discredited scientific discipline called eugenics. The name comes from words meaning "well born."

Eugenics started in the late nineteenth century with the writings of Francis Galton, a cousin of famed evolution pioneer Charles Darwin. Galton believed that intelligence and social behavior were inherited. He said that people should try to control those characteristics by selective breeding, the same kind of "genetic engineering" that humans have used to improve domestic plants and animals for thousands of years. In other words, people with desirable characteristics should be encouraged to have children. Those who had undesirable traits should be discouraged or even prevented from doing so. In 1872 Galton wrote:

> It may become to be avowed as a paramount duty, to antic-ipate the slow and stubborn process of natural selection, by endeavouring to breed out feeble constitutions [body types], and petty and ignoble instincts, and to breed in those which are vigorous and noble and social.[119]

Around the beginning of the twentieth century, Galton formed a Eugenics Society in Britain to carry out these aims. Similar groups were established in the United States and Germany. By the late 1920s, twenty-four states in the United States had passed eugenics laws. These laws required people considered unfit to reproduce,

Nineteenth-century explorer and anthropologist Francis Galton believed that people should try to engage in selective breeding to improve themselves, and people with undesirable traits should be prevented from having children. Some people believe that today's genetic research is ultimately aiming toward this same goal.

such as the developmentally disabled, to be forcibly sterilized, or made unable to have children. The Nazi government of Germany carried eugenics even further in the 1930s and early 1940s. It tried to wipe out the genes of what it saw as inferior races by killing all the members of those groups.

Redefining Humanity

One of the chief problems with eugenics was that its standards were defined by a very limited group of people: members of the white, Anglo-Saxon, upper and middle classes. The physical and mental characteristics they chose as desirable were ones that they themselves had. Traits they labeled undesirable belonged to other races or classes.

Present-day critics fear that if germ-line genes are altered in an attempt to "improve" the human race, the alterations would be chosen by that same limited group. British geneticist William Cookson describes the possible consequences of such a "new eugenics" amusingly:

> A . . . disdain for people who can make things work has . . . been common in British educators for most of this century. . . . If the eugenicists had their way we would be left with . . .

[nothing but] prim, precise individuals with neat beards . . . , competing bloodily for membership of Mensa [a club limited to people with high scores on intelligence tests] while industry ceased to function and crops rotted in the fields.[120]

The specter of germ-line gene changes made on a racist or classist basis is no laughing matter to many. "There can be no question of science 'improving' the human species, in the sense of some people being of greater value than others," Noelle Lenoir, president of the United Nations Educational, Scientific, and Cultural Organization's International Bioethics Committee, said in a 1994 interview.

We must make sure that the folly of genetic purity does not take over from the folly of racial purity. The idea of "scientifically" manufacturing a set of people exclusively composed of individuals with certain characteristics must be outlawed because it runs counter to the dignity of human beings.[121]

Germ-line gene alteration need not follow the path of eugenics, however. Some of its supporters feel sure that it will not. William Cookson, for instance, maintains:

The new genetics will not produce a new racism or a new wave of prejudice against those perceived to be genetically disadvantaged. Indeed, in many instances it will show such prejudice to be irrational.[122]

As long as genetic changes are not made along racist or classist lines, some supporters feel that attempts to "improve" the human germ line might not be unethical, even if such changes went beyond removing genes that cause serious illness. "Would it really be so bad if we added genes for height to small people, or for hair to the bald, or good eyesight to the myopic [nearsighted]? Probably not,"[123] writes Walter Bodmer. James Watson, codiscoverer of the structure of DNA, has written,

A lot of people say they're worried about changing our genetic instructions, but those [instructions] are just a product of evolution designed to adapt us for certain conditions that may not exist today. . . . [So] why not make ourselves a little better suited for survival?[124]

Artificial Twins

A final kind of gene alteration that worries many people today is the possible cloning of human beings. Clones are two or more living things that have exactly the same genes. Identical twins are natural clones. Although making artificial clones does not involve changing individual genes, it is a kind of genetic engineering. As such, it arouses many of the same fears as other manipulations of human genes.

No human clones have been made yet, but breakthroughs in this field are coming so quickly that such a feat may well become possible in the next ten, or even five, years. In January 1997, for instance, Scottish geneticist Ian Wilmut announced that he and his research team had produced a cloned lamb, which they called Dolly, from a single breast cell of an adult ewe (female sheep).

Why would people want to make clones of themselves or their children? One possible answer is "spare parts." Organs harvested from brainless clones might be the best answer to the current shortage of human organs for transplantation. People who receive transplants today have to take powerful drugs for the rest of their lives to keep their immune systems from attacking the "foreign" transplanted tissue. Organs from a clone, however, would not seem foreign to the immune system because they would contain the same genes as the original person.

Cloned bodies might also be produced for scientific experimentation or for extraction of useful body chemicals, just as some genetically engineered animals are now. Genetics pioneer Erwin Chargaff has written,

> What I see coming is a gigantic slaughterhouse, a molecular Auschwitz [concentration camp], in which valuable

Dolly, the world's first sheep cloned from an adult sheep cell. Many ethicists are deeply troubled by such cloned animals, believing that scientists will now attempt to extend these breakthroughs to engineer human beings.

enzymes, hormones and so on will be extracted [from cloned bodies] instead of gold teeth.[125]

Cloning may also be used in a kind of indirect eugenics. Today some men of very high intelligence, including Nobel prize winners, have donated their sperm to sperm banks. Women can pay to have their eggs fertilized in the laboratory by these sperm, thus gaining a share of the men's supposedly superior genes for their children. If cloning became easy, cells carrying the genes of people deemed superior might be cloned and sold in a similar way. The existence of many such clones could, in effect, change the human germ line, because those clones could breed and spread their genes through the population.

Should Cloning Be Banned?

The idea of cloning humans frightens many people so much that they want to ban not only human cloning but all research related to it. Shortly after accounts of Ian Wilmut's cloned sheep appeared in the press, for example, President Bill Clinton ordered a ban on the use of federal funds to support any research likely to lead to human cloning. "Any discovery that touches upon human creation is not simply a matter of scientific inquiry," Clinton told a press conference on March 4, 1997. "It is a matter of morality and spirituality as well."[126] Ian Wilmut himself said he would "assist those who want to prohibit the use of this technique to produce a new person."[127]

On the other hand, Harold Varmus, director of the NIH, thinks society may eventually decide that cloning of humans is acceptable under rare circumstances. For example, when a couple cannot bear children and yet strongly want to have a child that is genetically related to them, a clone of one parent might be made. "Maybe there are some situations in which we would find it [human cloning] ethical,"[128] Varmus told a congressional committee early in 1997.

Even some scientists who disapprove of human cloning feel that banning all related research would be going too far. For example, Roger A. Pedersen, a professor of reproductive sciences at the University of California at San Francisco, stated in a letter to the *San Francisco Chronicle* on March 21, 1997, that he opposed human cloning because it "would negate the individuality of any deliberately cloned person."[129] At the same time, he said that research related to cloning carried out on human cells in the laboratory that were not allowed to develop into whole beings should continue. He believes that such research will shed light on cancer and other diseases by showing more about the role that genes play in them.

In June 1997 the National Bioethics Advisory Commission came to a similar conclusion. Partly opposing President Clinton's recommendation of a complete ban on cloning-related research, it urged that Congress make laws that would permit privately financed scientists to make cloned human embryos (living things in a very early stage of development) for research purposes but not allow them to develop into babies. (Scientists first experimentally created cloned human embryos—but did not let them develop—in 1993.) The commission did, however, urge laws that would ban the creation of cloned human *children* for at least three years.

A Need for Education

People disagree about the best way to prevent possible future abuses of genetic engineering. Some want laws to ban certain kinds of human gene alteration, such as cloning. Others want to outlaw certain kinds of abuse, such as discrimination on the basis of results from genetic testing. Some want committees appointed by the government or by scientific organizations to approve new gene therapy experiments or to consider the ethical, social, and legal implications

of advances in the field. "People get reassurance by knowing that there is a special body for overseeing genetics at the national level,"[130] Arthur Caplan told an interviewer in 1996.

Most bioethicists agree, however, that a key factor in fighting both potential abuses and unfounded fears will be better public education about genetics. People need to learn, for instance, the difference between somatic and germ-line gene therapy. They need to learn the difference between the carrier of a genetic defect and someone who actually suffers from the disease caused by that defect. Karl A. Drlica writes, "Sophisticated knowledge by the public is needed to fully grasp the implications of genetic issues. . . . Effective control over genetics is more likely to come from superior knowledge."[131]

Conclusion ■

Placing the Stop Sign

B IOETHICISTS AND CITIZENS in the twenty-first century are likely to face some of the toughest ethical issues ever. As the world's population continues to grow and more people in industrialized countries enter old age, questions about how health care will be distributed and paid for will become even harder to answer and more painful than they are today. As technology's power to extend life increases, it will raise questions not only of cost but of quality of life: When is life no longer worth living? And who should decide? Breakthroughs in medical testing and, perhaps, in organ transplantation between species will bring up questions about the fate of thousands or even millions of animals. New developments in gene therapy will raise questions about the nature and fate of the human species itself.

Each of these issues involves not just one question or set of choices but many. Each choice that people make affects others. This is why dealing with such complex issues, and determining where to place a stop sign on the slippery slope of potential decisions, is so hard. Thoughtful, rational answers to these difficult bioethical questions will become possible only if people overcome three barriers: lack of education, dependence on emotion, and unwillingness to discuss the issues openly.

In the past, people usually could answer ethical questions, at least to their own satisfaction, by referring to things they knew well, such as religious or cultural traditions or their own life experiences. In the coming century, however, many bioethicists feel that these old guides will not be enough. Because so many of tomorrow's bioethical dilemmas will arise out of advances in science, people will be able to make intelligent choices about these issues only if they understand science much better than most now do. Only then will they know what to fear and what not to. For example, an editorial in the British medical journal *Lancet* commented:

> It is curious how frightened people are of genetic engineering compared with, say, child abuse. Genetic engineering has so far damaged no one. By contrast, smoking, AIDS, drugs and alcohol have caused massive damage to children [before birth]. . . . What one needs is an educated public. They need to be sufficiently DNA literate.[132]

When an animal is frightened, it may lash out blindly. Human beings often do the same. Faced with new ideas that they do not completely understand, many people "think" with only their emotions. They hear certain words or read about certain incidents that stir up

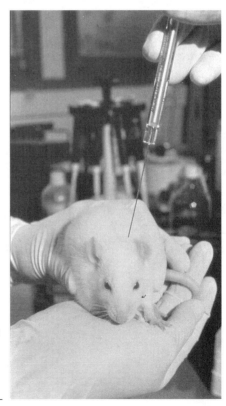

A laboratory mouse is given an injection as part of research on possible gene therapy for Alzheimer's disease, which causes severe memory loss in afflicted people. Many scientists view people's fear of genetic engineering as little more than ignorance.

strong feelings, and they make decisions based only on those feelings. Groups that want people to reach certain decisions sometimes take advantage of these emotional reactions or even produce them deliberately. More thoughtful leaders, however, decry such dependence on emotions. Animal rights activist Henry Spira, for example, calls the "black-and-white, saints-and-sinners approach" that has often marked the debate between animal rights protesters and biomedical researchers a "deplorable state of affairs."[133]

If a frightened animal feels that defending itself is hopeless, it will try to hide. People, too, often try to hide from questions that frighten them. They refuse to discuss certain problems or, sometimes, even to admit that the problems exist. As a result, decisions about those problems are made piecemeal, often as much by actions that are *not* taken as by deliberate choices. When decisions are made deliberately, they may be made in secret by the few people who are determined enough to tackle them. Those people may not represent the views of society as a whole.

If people want their views to be represented in decisions about bioethical issues, they must be willing to stop hiding and begin dis-

---

Animal rights activists protest animal research. Discussion of controversial issues like this often involves more emotion than reason.

cussing these painful subjects openly. Thomas A. Shannon of the Worcester Polytechnic Institute in Massachusetts writes, "What PAS [physician-assisted suicide] needs more than anything is debate. . . . Only a genuine national, popular debate can benefit the resolution of this issue."[134] Similarly, Melinda Beck writes in *Newsweek* that any choices about health care rationing "will be painful choices, but if we continue to hide from them, we will never make them wisely."[135]

In deciding where to draw lines on the slippery slopes of bioethics, people must be willing both to talk and to listen. They must be willing to use both their minds and their hearts. Only then will they have a chance of reaching wise decisions about the extremely complex medical issues that they, their children, and their grandchildren will face.

NOTES

Introduction: Down a Slippery Slope?

1. Quoted in Claudia Dreifuss, "Who Gets the Liver Transplant?" *New York Times Magazine*, December 15, 1996, p. 42.
2. Quoted in Dreifuss, "Liver Transplant," p. 42.
3. Quoted in Dreifuss, "Liver Transplant," p. 41.
4. Kathy A. Fackelmann, "DNA Dilemmas," *Science News,* December 17, 1994, p. 408.
5. Quoted in Victoria Sherrow, *Bioethics and High-Tech Medicine.* New York: Holt/Twenty-First Century Books, 1996, p. 12.

Chapter 1: How Should Health Care Be Allocated?

6. Quoted in Sherrow, *Bioethics and High-Tech Medicine,* p. 120.
7. Quoted in Melinda Beck, "Rationing Health Care," *Newsweek,* June 27, 1994, p. 35.
8. Harriet A. Washington, "Rationing the Right to Survive," *Emerge,* February 1994, pp. 71–72.
9. Daniel Callahan, "Rationing Health Care Is Effective and Necessary," in Carol Wekesser, ed., *Health Care in America: Opposing Viewpoints.* San Diego: Greenhaven Press, 1994, p. 190.
10. Quoted in Wekesser, *Health Care in America,* p. 188.
11. Quoted in Sherrow, *Bioethics and High-Tech Medicine,* p. 111.
12. Quoted in Sherrow, *Bioethics and High-Tech Medicine,* p. 111.
13. David M. Eddy, "Health System Reform," *Journal of the American Medical Association,* July 27, 1994, p. 327.
14. David M. Eddy, "Rationing Resources While Improving Quality,"

Journal of the American Medical Association, September 14, 1994, p. 823.

15. Eddy, "Rationing Resources," pp. 818, 820.

16. Callahan, "Rationing Health Care," p. 187.

17. Quoted in Gina Kolata, "Survival Odds to Dictate Which Patients Get Livers," *San Francisco Chronicle,* November 15, 1996.

18. Quoted in Wekesser, *Health Care in America,* p. 194.

19. Quoted in William Carlsen, "Doctor to Confess Role in Man's Death," *San Francisco Chronicle,* April 5, 1997.

20. Quoted in Carlsen, "Doctor to Confess."

21. James F. Childress, "Who Shall Live When Not All Can Live?" in Rem B. Edwards and Glenn C. Graber, eds., *Bioethics.* San Diego: Harcourt Brace Jovanovich, 1988, p. 721.

22. Childress, "Who Shall Live?" p. 721.

23. Childress, "Who Shall Live?" p. 722.

24. Quoted in Sherrow, *Bioethics and High-Tech Health Care,* p. 122.

25. Eddy, "Rationing Resources," p. 823.

26. Childress, "Who Shall Live?" p. 719.

27. Quoted in Daniel Jussim, *Medical Ethics.* New York: Julian Messner, 1991, p. 93.

28. Childress, "Who Shall Live?" p. 717.

29. Steven A. Schroeder, "Rationing Medical Care—A Comparative Perspective," *New England Journal of Medicine,* October 20, 1994, p. 1089.

30. Arthur L. Caplan, "Current Ethical Issues in Organ Procurement and Transplantation," *Journal of the American Medical Association,* December 7, 1994, p. 1709.

31. Quoted in Edwards and Graber, *Bioethics,* p. 728.

32. Washington, "Rationing the Right to Survive," p. 71.

33. C. Everett Koop, "Manage with Care," *Time,* Fall 1996, p. 69.

34. Quoted in Todd Simmons, "Mangled Care," *Advocate,* May 14, 1996, p. 33.

35. Council on Ethical and Judicial Affairs, American Medical Association, "Ethical Issues in Managed Care," *Journal of the American Medical Association,* January 25, 1995, p. 333.

36. Carolyn M. Clancy and Howard Brody, "Managed Care: Jekyll or Hyde?" *Journal of the American Medical Association,* January

25, 1995, p. 338.

37. Clancy and Brody, "Managed Care: Jekyll or Hyde?" p. 338.

38. Quoted in Edwards and Graber, *Bioethics,* p. 727.

Chapter 2: Should Doctors Ever Hasten Patients' Deaths?

39. Quoted in Richard Jerome, "Post Mortem," *People,* September 16, 1996, p. 53.

40. Quoted in Jerome, "Post Mortem," p. 54.

41. Joseph P. Shapiro with David Bowermaster, "Death on Trial," *U.S. News & World Report,* April 25, 1994, p. 34.

42. Shapiro with Bowermaster, "Death on Trial," p. 34.

43. Quoted in Jussim, *Medical Ethics,* p. 66.

44. Quoted in Jeffrey Rosen, "What Right to Die?" *New Republic,* June 24, 1996, p. 29.

45. Quoted in Steve Hallock, "Physician-Assisted Suicide: 'Slippery Slope' or Civil Right?" *Humanist,* July/August 1996, p. 8.

46. Quoted in M. L. Tina Stevens, "What *Quinlan* Can Tell Kevorkian About the Right to Die," *Humanist,* March/April 1997, p. 12.

47. Quoted in George J. Annas, "The Promised End—Constitutional Aspects of Physician-Assisted Suicide," *New England Journal of Medicine,* August 29, 1996, p. 683.

48. Marcia Angell, "The Supreme Court and Physician-Assisted Suicide—The Ultimate Right," *New England Journal of Medicine,* January 2, 1997, p. 50.

49. Robert P. George and William C. Porth Jr., "Death, Be Not Proud," *National Review,* June 26, 1995, p. 50.

50. Quoted in William Carlsen, "When Patients Choose to Die," *San Francisco Chronicle,* June 3, 1996.

51. Quoted in "Most Justices Dubious About Assisted Suicide," *San Francisco Chronicle,* January 9, 1997.

52. Quoted in Harriet Chiang, "States Can Ban Assisted Suicide," *San Francisco Chronicle,* June 27, 1997.

53. Quoted in Edwards and Graber, *Bioethics,* p. 40.

54. Angell, "The Supreme Court and Physician-Assisted Suicide," p. 52.

55. David Orentlicher, "The Legalization of Physician-Assisted Suicide," *New England Journal of Medicine,* August 29, 1996, p. 664.

56. Quoted in Hallock, "Physician-Assisted Suicide," p. 10.

57. Quoted in Dreifuss, "Liver Transplant," p. 44.

58. Angell, "The Supreme Court and Physician-Assisted Suicide," p. 51.

59. Quoted in Peter J. Bernardi, "Is Death a Right?" *Christianity Today*, May 20, 1996, p. 30.

60. Quoted in Sherrow, *Bioethics and High-Tech Medicine,* p. 105.

61. Quoted in David Van Biema, "Is There a Right to Die?" *Time,* January 13, 1997, p. 61.

62. George and Porth, "Death, Be Not Proud," p. 52.

63. Quoted in Paul Wilkes, "The Next Pro-Lifers," *New York Times Magazine,* July 21, 1996, p. 26.

64. Paul J. van der Maas et al., "Euthanasia, Physician-Assisted Suicide, and Other Medical Practices Involving the End of Life in the Netherlands, 1990–1995," *New England Journal of Medicine,* November 28, 1996, p. 1705.

65. Anthony L. Back et al., "Physician-Assisted Suicide and Euthanasia in Washington State," *Journal of the American Medical Association,* March 27, 1996, p. 924.

66. Leon R. Kass and Nelson Lund, "Courting Death: Assisted Suicide, Doctors, and the Law," *Commentary,* December 1996, p. 28.

67. Stephen L. Carter, "Rush to a Lethal Judgment," *New York Times Magazine,* July 21, 1996, p. 29.

Chapter 3: Should Animals Be Used in Medical Research and Testing?

68. Quoted in Terry O'Neill, ed., *Biomedical Ethics: Opposing Viewpoints.* San Diego: Greenhaven Press, 1994, p. 209.

69. Quoted in O'Neill, *Biomedical Ethics,* p. 209.

70. Quoted in O'Neill, *Biomedical Ethics,* p. 209.

71. Donald J. Barnes, "A Shadow on the Face of Science," *The Animals' Voice,* April–June 1995, p. 42.

72. Quoted in O'Neill, *Biomedical Ethics,* p. 211.

73. Carl Cohen, "The Case for the Use of Animals in Biomedical Research," in Robert M. Baird and Stuart E. Rosenbaum, eds., *Ani-*

mal Experimentation: The Moral Issues. Buffalo, NY: Prometheus Books, 1991, p. 109.

74. Quoted in Baird and Rosenbaum, *Animal Experimentation,* p. 9.

75. Jean Bethke Elshtain, "Animal Research Is Unnecessary," in O'Neill, *Biomedical Ethics,* p. 207.

76. John G. Hubbell, "Animal Rights Protesters Disrupt Valuable Research," in O'Neill, *Biomedical Ethics,* p. 210.

77. Quoted in O'Neill, *Biomedical Ethics,* p. 212.

78. Richard McCourt, "Model Patients," *Discover,* August 1990, p. 36.

79. Barnes, "A Shadow on the Face of Science," p. 41.

80. Quoted in Barnes, "A Shadow on the Face of Science," p. 42.

81. Quoted in Sunni Bloyd, *Animal Rights.* San Diego: Lucent Books, 1990, p. 38.

82. Bernard E. Rollin, "The Use and Abuse of Animals in Research," in Edwards and Graber, *Bioethics,* p. 235.

83. Quoted in Christine Gorman, "What's It Worth to Find a Cure?" *Time,* July 8, 1996, p. 53.

84. Steven I. Simmons, "Respect for All Life Is the Real Cure," *Animals' Agenda,* September/October 1996, p. 43.

85. Carol Grunewald, "Genetic Research on Animals Oversteps Human Rights," in O'Neill, *Biomedical Ethics,* p. 245.

86. Caroline Murphy, "Genetic Research on Animals Will Benefit Humanity," in O'Neill, *Biomedical Ethics,* p. 242.

87. Arthur L. Caplan, "Humans Should Be Allowed to Receive Animal Organ Transplants," in O'Neill, *Biomedical Ethics,* p. 225.

88. James Lindemann Nelson, "Humans Should Not Be Allowed to Receive Animal Organs," in O'Neill, *Biomedical Ethics,* p. 232.

89. Quoted in Bloyd, *Animal Rights,* pp. 37–38.

90. Quoted in Laurence Pringle, *The Animal Rights Controversy.* San Diego: Harcourt Brace Jovanovich, 1989, p. 71.

91. Rollin, "Use and Abuse of Animals," p. 238.

92. Martin L. Stephens, "A Current View of Vivisection: Animal Research in America," *Animals' Agenda,* September/October 1996, p. 24.

93. Jessica Szymczyk, "Animals, Vegetables and Minerals,"

Newsweek, August 14, 1995, p. 10.

94. Stephens, "A Current View of Vivisection," p. 22.

95. Stephens, "A Current View of Vivisection," p. 21.

96. Caplan, "Humans Should Be Allowed," pp. 229–30.

97. Henry Spira, "What's Really Happening in Alternatives?" *Animals' Voice,* January–March 1994, p. 10.

98. Quoted in O'Neill, *Biomedical Ethics,* p. 212.

99. Elshtain, "Animal Research Is Unnecessary," p. 206.

100. Quoted in Stephen Schwartz, "Exploring Our Kinship with the Apes," *San Francisco Chronicle,* December 15, 1996.

101. Rollin, "Use and Abuse of Animals," p. 232.

Chapter 4: Should Human Genes Be Altered?

102. W. French Anderson, "Gene Therapy," *Scientific American,* September 1995, p. 124.

103. W. French Anderson, "Genetic Engineering Should Be Restricted to Medical Therapy," in O'Neill, *Biomedical Ethics,* pp. 276–77.

104. Quoted in Richard Golob and Eric Brus, eds., *The Almanac of Science and Technology.* Boston: Harcourt Brace Jovanovich, 1990, p. 120.

105. Quoted in Golob and Brus, *The Almanac of Science and Technology,* p. 121.

106. Clifford Grobstein and Michael Flower, "Gene Therapy: Proceed with Caution," in Edwards and Graber, *Bioethics,* p. 693.

107. Quoted in Andrew Kimbrell, *The Human Body Shop.* San Francisco: HarperSanFrancisco, 1993, p. 68.

108. Karl A. Drlica, *Double-Edged Sword: The Promises and Risks of the Genetic Revolution.* Reading, MA: Addison-Wesley/Helix, 1994, p. 148.

109. *Economist,* "Genetic Engineering Should Be Unrestricted," in O'Neill, *Biomedical Ethics,* p. 272.

110. Quoted in Janet Basu, "Genetic Roulette," *Stanford Today,* November/December 1996, p. 42.

111. Walter Bodmer and Robin McKie, *The Book of Man.* New York: Scribner, 1994, p. 240.

112. Bodmer and McKie, *The Book of Man,* p. 244.

113. Grobstein and Flower, "Gene Therapy," p. 693.

114. Quoted in David Suzuki and Peter Knudtson, *Genethics: The Ethics of Engineering Life*. Toronto: Stoddart, 1988, p. 181.

115. Suzuki and Knudtson, *Genethics*, p. 181.

116. *Economist*, "Genetic Engineering Should Be Unrestricted," p. 273.

117. Quoted in Robin Marantz Henig, "Dr. Anderson's Gene Machine," *New York Times Magazine*, March 31, 1991, p. 34.

118. Quoted in Sherrow, *Bioethics and High-Tech Medicine*, p. 41.

119. Quoted in William Cookson, *The Gene Hunters*. London: Aurum Press, 1994, p. 191.

120. Cookson, *The Gene Hunters*, p. 194.

121. Quoted in Bahgat Elnadi, and Adel Rifaat, "Noelle Lenoir," *UNESCO Courier*, September 1994, p. 8.

122. Cookson, *The Gene Hunters*, p. 195.

123. Bodmer and McKie, *The Book of Man*, p. 246.

124. Quoted in O'Neill, *Biomedical Ethics*, p. 259.

125. Quoted in O'Neill, *Biomedical Ethics*, p. 256.

126. Quoted in David Perlman and Charles Petit, "Clinton Bans Human Clone Funding," *San Francisco Chronicle*, March 5, 1997.

127. Quoted in "Clone Scientist Supports Ban on Technique," *San Francisco Chronicle*, March 10, 1997.

128. Quoted in "Don't Rule Out Human Clones, Says NIH Director," *San Francisco Chronicle*, March 6, 1997.

129. Roger Pedersen, "Breakthrough's Positive Implications," *San Francisco Chronicle*, March 21, 1997.

130. Quoted in Vincent Kiernan, "Fears Mount for Gene Scrutiny as Watchdog Faces Axe," *New Scientist*, June 8, 1996, p. 10.

131. Drlica, *Double-Edged Sword*, p. 151.

Conclusion: Placing the Stop Sign

132. Quoted in Bodmer and McKie, *The Book of Man*, p. 246.

133. Spira, "What's Really Happening in Alternatives?" p. 10.

134. Thomas A. Shannon, "Physician-Assisted Suicide: Ten Questions," *Commonweal*, June 1, 1996, p. 16.

135. Beck, "Rationing Health Care," p. 35.

GLOSSARY

autonomy: The value of self-determination or freedom to make one's own decisions.

beneficence: The value of doing the right thing and promoting well-being.

bioethics (biomedical ethics): The application of ethics to issues in health care and medical research.

carrier: Someone who has one copy of a defective gene and can transmit a genetic disease but will not suffer from the disease.

clone: An exact genetic duplicate of a living thing.

coma: A state of deep unconsciousness; sometimes called persistent vegetative state.

cystic fibrosis: A serious disease, caused by a defective gene, that damages the lungs.

depression: A mental illness marked by deep unhappiness and feelings of worthlessness.

DNA: Deoxyribonucleic acid, the chemical from which genes are made.

ethics: The philosophy of good and evil, right and wrong.

eugenics: A now-discredited scientific discipline that urged improvement of humans through selective breeding.

euthanasia: Killing for the purpose of ending pain and suffering.

fidelity: The value of keeping promises and contracts.

gene: A unit of hereditary material in a cell that codes for one characteristic or one body chemical.

gene therapy: Changing genes for the purpose of curing or preventing disease.

genetic engineering: Artificially changing genes or transferring genes from one kind of living thing to another.

genetics: The branch of biology that studies genes and inheritance of characteristics.

germ-line genes: Genes contained in the sex cells (eggs or sperm) and passed on to offspring.

hormone: A body chemical that sends messages between cells.

hospice: An institution that specializes in care of the dying, relieving their discomfort without trying to cure them.

immune system: The system of cells and chemicals that defends the body against disease by attacking microbes and other foreign material.

LD50: Lethal Dose 50, a test that measures how poisonous a substance is by determining how much of the substance is needed to kill 50 percent of a group of animals given it.

managed health care organization: An organization that both pays for and provides health care to its members.

Medicaid: A health care insurance program for poor people in the United States, funded by federal and state governments.

nonmaleficence: The value of not doing harm to others.

physician-assisted suicide: Suicide for which a doctor knowingly provides the means, such as a lethal prescription.

prenatal: Before birth.

primary care: Basic health care, usually administered by a single doctor who sees a patient on a regular basis.

primate: A monkey, ape, or human being.

rescue medicine: Medicine that focuses on treating disease after it develops.

respirator: A device that forces the body to breathe.

sickle-cell disease: A serious blood disease caused by a defective gene.

side effect: An undesirable effect of a drug or medical treatment.

somatic cell therapy: Gene therapy that affects only the cells of an individual's body; the changed genes are not passed on to the person's offspring.

terminal illness: An illness that is expected to kill a person in six months or less.

trait: An inherited characteristic.

veracity: The value of truthfulness.

vivisection: Cutting into or invading the body of a living thing for the purpose of scientific research.

ORGANIZATIONS TO CONTACT

American Fund for Alternatives to Animal Research
175 W. 12th St., No. 16-G
New York, NY 10011
(212) 989-8073

This organization supports the search for alternatives to the use of animals in medical research. It offers press releases and other material.

Americans for Medical Progress Educational Foundation
421 King St., Suite 401
Alexandria, VA 22314-3121
(703) 836-9595
e-mail: ampef@aol.com
Internet: http://www.ampef.org/index.html

This group supports the use of animals in medical research and opposes animal rights groups. It offers educational material.

American Society for the Prevention of Cruelty to Animals
424 E. 92nd St.
New York, NY 10128-6804
(212) 876-7700
Internet: http://www.aspca.org

This large traditional animal welfare organization would like to see use of animals in medical research minimized and treatment of laboratory animals improved.

American Society of Human Genetics

9650 Rockville Pike
Bethesda, MD 20814-3998
(301) 571-1825
e-mail: society@genetics.faseb.org
Internet: http://www.faseb

This group, consisting of scientists who study human genetics, may have educational material or bibliographies related to this field.

The Bioetech Chronicles

Internet: http://www.gene.com/AE/AB/BC/index.html

This website contains information about genetic engineering/biotechnology and its pioneer scientists, including some information on gene therapy.

Choice in Dying

200 Varick St.
New York, NY 10014-4810
(212) 366-5540
e-mail: cid@choices.org
Internet: http://www.choices.org

This group supports terminally ill people's right to request death. It provides educational literature supporting this point of view.

Foundation for Biomedical Research

818 Connecticut Ave. NW, Suite 303
Washington, DC 20006
(202) 457-0654
Internet: http://www.fbresearch.org

This group supports humane use of animals in medical research and provides educational material.

Hastings Center

255 Elm Rd.
Briarcliff Manor, NY 10510

(914) 762-8500

Internet: http://www.cpn.org/sections/affiliates/hastings_
center.html

This is a well-known center for research in bioethics.

Hemlock Society USA
Box 101810
Denver, CO 80250-1810
(303) 639-10202
Internet: http://www2.privatei.com/hemlock/general.html

This group supports the right to die and provides educational literature supporting this point of view.

Humane Society of the United States
2100 L St. NW
Washington, DC 20037
(202) 452-1100
Internet: http://www.hsus.org

This traditional animal welfare organization is opposed to most use
of animals in medical research and works to improve treatment of
animals used in research.

International Anti-Euthanasia Task Force
Box 760
Steubenville, OH 43952
(614) 282-3810
Internet: http://www.iaetf.org

This organization opposes physician-assisted suicide and euthanasia
and distributes educational packets supporting its point of view.

International Center for Bioethics
2960 Vecino Dr.
Sacramento, CA 95833
(916) 921-2205

This center for bioethical research publishes a book, *First Do No Harm.*

People for the Ethical Treatment of Animals (PETA)
Box 42516
Washington, DC 20015
(202) 770-7444
Internet: http://www.envirolink.org/arrs/peta/index.html

This group opposes the use of animals in research and testing and distributes educational literature supporting this point of view.

United Network for Organ Sharing
1100 Boulders Pkwy., Suite 500
Box 13770
Richmond, VA 23225
(804) 330-8500
Internet: http://www.ew3.att.net/unos

This group oversees distribution of organs for transplant in the United States. It may offer literature describing its methods of allocating organs, statistics related to organ donation, and the like.

FOR FURTHER READING

Jeffrey Finn and Eliot L. Marshall, *Medical Ethics.* New York: Chelsea House, 1990. For young adults. Includes chapters on reproduction, organ transplantation, physician-assisted death, and allocation of health care resources.

Daniel Jussim, *Medical Ethics.* New York: Julian Messner, 1991. For young adults. Includes chapters on abortion, reproduction, sick babies, physician-assisted death, and organ transplants.

Terry O'Neill, ed., *Biomedical Ethics: Opposing Viewpoints.* San Diego: Greenhaven Press, 1994. Anthology of articles with opposing viewpoints on biomedical ethics issues. Includes sections on experimentation on humans and animals, organ transplants, fetal tissue research, reproductive technologies, and gene therapy.

Laurence Pringle, *The Animal Rights Controversy.* San Diego: Harcourt Brace Jovanovich, 1989. For young adults. Includes history and philosophy of the animal rights movement and a chapter on animals in research.

Victoria Sherrow, *Bioethics and High-Tech Medicine.* New York: Holt/Twenty-First Century Books, 1996. For young adults. Includes chapters on gene therapy, genetic testing, reproduction, organ transplants, physician-assisted death, and allocation of health care resources.

Carol Wekesser, ed., *Health Care in America: Opposing Viewpoints.* San Diego: Greenhaven Press, 1994. Anthology of articles with opposing viewpoints on health care issues. Includes essays on health care rationing.

Lisa Yount, *Genetics and Genetic Engineering.* New York: Facts On File, 1997 [forthcoming]. For young adults. Describes key discoveries in the field, with some consideration of ethical issues.

WORKS CONSULTED

W. French Anderson, "Gene Therapy," *Scientific American,* September 1995, pp. 124–28.

Marcia Angell, "The Supreme Court and Physician-Assisted Suicide—The Ultimate Right," *New England Journal of Medicine,* January 2, 1997, pp. 50–53.

George J. Annas, "The Promised End—Constitutional Aspects of Physician-Assisted Suicide," *New England Journal of Medicine,* August 29, 1996, pp. 683–87.

Anthony L. Back et al., "Physician-Assisted Suicide and Euthanasia in Washington State," *Journal of the American Medical Association,* March 27, 1996, pp. 919–925.

Robert M. Baird and Stuart E. Rosenbaum, eds., *Animal Experimentation: The Moral Issues.* Buffalo, NY: Prometheus Books, 1991.

Donald J. Barnes, "A Shadow on the Face of Science," *The Animals' Voice,* April–June 1995, pp. 41–44.

Janet Basu, "Genetic Roulette," *Stanford Today,* November/December 1996, pp. 38–43.

Melinda Beck, "Rationing Health Care," *Newsweek,* June 27, 1994, pp. 30-35.

Peter J. Bernardi, "Is Death a Right?" *Christianity Today,* May 20, 1996, pp. 29–30.

Sunni Bloyd, *Animal Rights.* San Diego: Lucent Books, 1990.

Walter Bodmer and Robin McKie, *The Book of Man.* New York: Scribner, 1994.

Arthur L. Caplan, "Current Ethical Issues in Organ Procurement and Transplantation," *Journal of the American Medical Association,* December 7, 1994, pp. 1708–1709.

William Carlsen, "Doctor to Confess Role in Man's Death," *San Francisco Chronicle,* April 5, 1997.

William Carlsen, "When Patients Choose to Die," *San Francisco Chronicle,* June 3, 1996.

Stephen L. Carter, "Rush to a Lethal Judgment," *New York Times Magazine,* July 21, 1996, pp. 28–29.

Harriet Chiang, "States Can Ban Assisted Suicide," *San Francisco Chronicle,* June 27, 1997.

Carolyn M. Clancy and Howard Brody, "Managed Care: Jekyll or Hyde?" *Journal of the American Medical Association,* January 25, 1996, pp. 338–39.

"Clone Scientist Supports Ban on Technique," *San Francisco Chronicle,* March 10, 1997.

William Cookson, *The Gene Hunters.* London: Aurum Press, 1994.

Council on Ethical and Judicial Affairs, American Medical Association, "Ethical Issues in Managed Care," *Journal of the American Medical Association,* January 25, 1995, pp. 330–35.

"Don't Rule Out Human Clones, Says NIH Director," *San Francisco Chronicle,* March 6, 1997.

Claudia Dreifuss, "Who Gets the Liver Transplant?" *New York Times Magazine,* December 15, 1996, pp. 41–45.

Karl A. Drlica, *Double-Edged Sword: The Promises and Risks of the Genetic Revolution.* Reading, MA: Addison-Wesley/Helix, 1994.

David M. Eddy, "Health System Reform," *Journal of the American Medical Association,* July 27, 1994, pp. 324–28.

David M. Eddy, "Rationing Resources While Improving Quality," *Journal of the American Medical Association,* September 14, 1994, pp. 817–24.

Rem B. Edwards and Glenn C. Graber, eds., *Bioethics.* San Diego: Harcourt Brace Jovanovich, 1988.

Bahgat Elnadi and Adel Rifaat, "Noelle Lenoir," *UNESCO Courier,* September 1994, pp. 5–8.

Kathy A. Fackelmann, "DNA Dilemmas," *Science News,* December 17, 1994, pp. 408–409.

Robert P. George and William C. Porth Jr., "Death, Be Not Proud," *National Review,* June 26, 1995, pp. 49–52.

Richard Golob and Eric Brus, eds., *The Almanac of Science and Technology.* Boston: Harcourt Brace Jovanovich, 1990.

Christine Gorman, "What's It Worth to Find a Cure?" *Time,* July 8, 1996, p. 53.

Steve Hallock, "Physician-Assisted Suicide: 'Slippery Slope' or Civil Right?" *Humanist,* July/August 1996, pp. 8–14.

Robin Marantz Henig, "Dr. Anderson's Gene Machine," *New York Times Magazine,* March 31, 1991, pp. 31–35.

Richard Jerome, "Post Mortem," *People,* September 16, 1996, pp. 52–55.

Leon R. Kass and Nelson Lund, "Courting Death: Assisted Suicide, Doctors, and the Law," *Commentary,* December 1996, pp. 17–29.

Jack Kevorkian, "A Modern Inquisition," *Utne Reader,* March/April 1995, pp. 42–45.

Vincent Kiernan, "Fears Mount for Gene Scrutiny as Watchdog Faces Axe," *New Scientist,* June 8, 1996, p. 10.

Andrew Kimbrell, *The Human Body Shop.* San Francisco: Harper-SanFrancisco, 1993.

Gina Kolata, "Survival Odds to Dictate Which Patients Get Livers," *San Francisco Chronicle,* November 15, 1996.

C. Everett Koop, "Manage with Care," *Time,* Fall 1996, p. 69.

Richard McCourt, "Model Patients," *Discover,* August 1990, pp. 36–41.

"Message in a Bottle," *Economist,* April 22, 1995, pp. 83–85.

"Most Justices Dubious About Assisted Suicide," *San Francisco Chronicle,* January 9, 1997.

David Orentlicher, "The Legalization of Physician-Assisted Suicide," *New England Journal of Medicine,* August 29, 1996, pp. 663–66.

Roger Pedersen, "Breakthrough's Positive Implications," *San Francisco Chronicle,* March 21, 1997.

David Perlman and Charles Petit, "Clinton Bans Human Clone Funding," *San Francisco Chronicle,* March 5, 1997.

Larry Reibstein, "Whose Right Is It?" *Newsweek,* January 20, 1997, p. 36.

Jeffrey Rosen, "What Right to Die?" *New Republic,* June 24, 1996, pp. 28–31.

Steven A. Schroeder, "Rationing Medical Care—A Comparative Perspective," *New England Journal of Medicine,* October 20, 1994, pp. 1089–1091.

Stephen Schwartz, "Exploring Our Kinship with the Apes," *San Francisco Chronicle,* December 15, 1996.

Thomas A. Shannon, "Physician-Assisted Suicide: Ten Questions," *Commonweal,* June 1, 1996, pp. 16–17.

Joseph P. Shapiro with David Bowermaster, "Death on Trial," *U.S. News & World Report,* April 25, 1994, pp. 31-39.

Steven I. Simmons, "Respect for All Life Is the Real Cure," *Animals' Agenda,* September/October 1996, pp. 42-43.

Todd Simmons, "Mangled Care," *Advocate,* May 14, 1996, pp. 31–34

Henry Spira, "What's Really Happening in Alternatives?" *Animals' Voice,* January–March 1994, pp. 10–11.

Martin L. Stephens, "A Current View of Vivisection: Animal Research in America," *Animals' Agenda,* September/October 1996, pp. 20-25.

M. L. Tina Stevens, "What *Quinlan* Can Tell Kevorkian About the Right to Die," *Humanist,* March/April 1997, pp. 10–15.

David Suzuki and Peter Knudtson, *Genethics: The Ethics of Engineering Life.* Toronto: Stoddart, 1988.

Jessica Szymczyk, "Animals, Vegetables and Minerals," *Newsweek,* August 14, 1995, p. 10.

David Van Biema, "Is There a Right to Die?" *Time,* January 13, 1997, pp. 60–61.

Paul J. van der Maas et al., "Euthanasia, Physician-Assisted Suicide, and Other Medical Practices Involving the End of Life in the Netherlands, 1990–1995," *New England Journal of Medicine,* November 28, 1996, pp. 1699–1705.

Karin Vergoth, "Guinea Pigs," *Psychology Today,* November/ December 1995, p. 21.

Harriet A. Washington, "Rationing the Right to Survive," *Emerge,* February 1994, pp. 70–72.

Paul Wilkes, "The Next Pro-Lifers," *New York Times Magazine,* July 21, 1996, pp. 22–27, 42.

INDEX

PICTURE CREDITS

ABOUT THE AUTHOR

Lisa Yount earned a bachelor's degree with honors in English and creative writing from Stanford University. She has a lifelong interest in biology and medicine. She has been a professional writer and editor for more than twenty-five years, producing educational materials, magazine articles, and over twenty books for young people. Her books for Lucent include *Pesticides, Memory,* and (with Harry Henderson) *Twentieth Century Science.* She lives in El Cerrito, California, with her husband, a large library, and five cats.